NORTHUMBRIA
MOTOR
SERVICES

STEVE JOHNSON

AMBERLEY

Front cover: Northumbria's unmistakeable livery of grey, white and red with bold diagonal lines enlivens the picturesque village of Whittingham as Bristol LH 631 (VDV 125S) heads to Alnwick from Wooler. (David Beilby)

Rear cover: Morpeth bus station could usually be relied upon to produce a fine line-up of Northumbria vehicles. Here, in 1997, a typical line-up of Leylands and Bristols can be seen. Nearest the camera is Plaxton-bodied Leopard 229 (NDC 501W), followed by 544, 243, 563, 538, 624, 636, 576, 627 and 206. (Keith Gregory)

First published 2023

Amberley Publishing
The Hill, Stroud,
Gloucestershire, GL5 4EP

www.amberley-books.com

ISBN: 978 1 3981 1023 6 (print)
ISBN: 978 1 3981 1024 3 (ebook)

British Library Cataloguing in Publication Data.
A catalogue record for this book is available from the British Library.

Typeset in 10pt on 13pt Celeste.
Typesetting by SJmagic DESIGN SERVICES, India.
Printed in the UK.

CONTENTS

FOREWORD

In the mid-1980s bus transport in the UK was in uncertain times as government thinking was making it clear that a change from a nationalised industry to a privatised and deregulated environment were to be the order of the day. For some of us who had been in the industry a while, this was going to be a challenge. I had been one of the very first group of graduate management trainees of the National Bus Company in 1970, but many of my colleagues had been in the industry for many years more.

However, some of us saw this as an opportunity. We had been involved in an industry that had seen decades of managed decline of services since a peak in the early 1950s and experienced capital expenditure cutbacks that prevented new buses being purchased in recent times.

You'll see photos of buses of various size and shape in this book, but the industry is very much a people business. It carries lots of people every day, is the working environment of many hundreds of people and is a lifeline for many communities who rely on regular services.

So when it was clear that in 1986 there was to be a massive change, some of us wanted to try a different way of doing things, like really putting customer care as a major aspect of our business. We would ask people where they wanted to go and run buses when people wanted to use them – and in comfortable buses too. And we'd sell ourselves as a forward-looking company.

We also felt that those who worked in the industry should be respected more, as individuals who wanted to give our customers a better service and to be appreciated for it – at all levels in a company, whatever their role. Fortunately, I and three other like-minded individuals were able to do just that with the formation of Northumbria Motor Services. Initially a new National Bus Company subsidiary, we then bought it from the government as our own business with our own destiny in a competitive environment.

You'll read in this book how we managed to try our best to make something of a new start for our staff and customers. A radical new look for the buses, new ways of communicating with our staff and customers, and new buses with features that our customers told us they would like. We also looked to add to our business by expanding to secure a stronger future.

Many outside influences affect any business and you can make your own assessment about whether we made a difference despite those changes.

My thanks go to Steve Johnson for taking this look at Northumbria's lifetime and for his enthusiasm in compiling this snapshot of just one bus company in a changing industry. But mostly to my fellow directors and all the wonderful members of the Northumbria community who served all the thousands of passengers who used our buses and coaches.

Tony Kennan CBE
Retired Chairman and Commercial Director of Northumbria

INTRODUCTION

On a Saturday morning in September 1986, shortly after my twelfth birthday, I found myself in the front seat of the service 501 bus heading for Morpeth to see my grandparents. Our bus was 6228, not one of my favourites – I had no idea of types, but I didn't like these! I had however spotted a sticker saying NORTHUMBRIA on the side over the old UNITED name. At Alnwick bus station the bus filled up and I noticed all the other buses in the station also had the same NORTHUMBRIA sticker on them. A short fast run down the A1 in a Leyland Leopard might excite your average bus enthusiast today, but back then there was excitement of a different sort on the journey – one which all the passengers bought into. In a stroke of cunning devilment by the schedules department the southbound bus left Alnwick at about the same time as the northbound bus left Morpeth. This meant the meeting of the buses was timed to occur on the tiny roads adjacent to the A1 south of Newton on the Moor. A tight squeeze was almost inevitable. By the time we left Alnwick the bus was nearly full. A few more passengers joined us at Newton on the Moor and then we headed off towards Felton and the main event of the bus meet.

Today our driver was not in luck as we met the northbound 501 at just about the worst possible place – a corner on a single-track section. We stopped nose to nose as they worked out who was going to manoeuvre first. The more astonishing thing was what had met us. Instead of the usual drab red and white bus we were greeted by a dazzling spectacle in grey and white, with a huge diagonal red stripe across the front. People actually stopped speaking and stood up in their seats to get a better view. The classic northern line of 'eeh, that's a bobby dazzler' was heard a few seats back. Someone else confidently said 'That's a brand-new bus, Ethel.' This I knew was not true. My encyclopaedic knowledge of local bus numbers meant I knew their fleet numbers and registration numbers in the same way that my schoolfriends knew the football players of Newcastle or Liverpool. Bus 6260, NDC 504W, was most definitely not new; it had arrived a few years earlier, one of five. As the two buses shuffled forwards and back to try to pass each other, our driver in particular trying not to put a mark on the side of the bobby dazzler, we got a side view of 6260 where there was lots more diagonal red, white and grey paint with a huge NORTHUMBRIA fleet name down the side.

Sitting there gobsmacked at the vision in front of us was, unbeknownst to everyone, exactly the effect the new company was intending. Something new. Radical, different, perhaps even daring. A break from tradition. A change was afoot in England's northernmost county. Within twelve years it was all over and a national corporate identity was once again brought to our local buses, but for that brief period Northumberland had arguably the most distinctive vehicles of any large operator in Britain. The change went far deeper than mere new paintwork though as an innovative team of directors dared to do things differently and managed to fundamentally change the future direction of the British bus industry. This book tells the story of the remarkable operator that was Northumbria Motor Services, from formation in 1986 to the end in 1998.

I am deeply indebted to a number of people for their assistance in researching this book. Former Northumbria directors David Monaghan, Tony Kennan, John Fickling and Steve Noble gave freely of their time, thinking and knowledge and without them this book would never have got off the ground. Bruce Hugman of Hyphen Hayden and later EQUUS kindly gave me his insights into the design of the Northumbria brand. David Baxter, Bill Campbell, David Cook, Neil Hudson, David McGow, Steven Oliver and Tim Weatherup all made valuable contributions to the text. To all the photographers who kindly made their work available, particularly Martin and Bill Counter and David Beilby, who gave access to their wonderful rural shots. The Omnibus Society and The PSV Circle for access to their archives. To Connor Stait at Amberley for his patience with a new author. To my mum, Kathleen, for many wonderful childhood trips on buses and to my wife, Beth, for her unending patience. I thank you all most sincerely.

During the course of the production of this book I learned of the sad death of former Managing Director Steve Noble and photographer Bill Counter. With grateful thanks for their invaluable contributions, this book is dedicated to them.

For further technical fleet details, allocations, timetables, *Herald* articles and publicity images visit www.northumbriabuses.co.uk

1

BEFORE NORTHUMBRIA

Late in the afternoon of Thursday 12 July 1984 the then Secretary of State for Transport, Northumberland-born Nicholas Ridley, presented a white paper to Parliament entitled simply 'Buses'. Flanked by Prime Minister Margaret Thatcher, the Conservatives were by now into their second term and had recently won a landslide majority in the general election of 1983. Policies that promoted free-market competition and privatisation of nationalised companies were at the heart of their approach and so the contents of the white paper were hardly surprising.

Up until that point bus operators were granted licences to operate bus services and could challenge any other operator who wished to begin services in the same area. The Conservatives saw this approach as a hindrance to competition and one which was leading to higher fares and cuts to rural bus services. It was therefore proposed that bus services in Great Britain would become deregulated. This would in essence mean any operator, large or small, could register and operate a bus service regardless of whether this was in direct competition with another service or not.

Across England and Wales many bus services were provided by a network of operations that collectively made up the National Bus Company or NBC. From the North East (United Automobile and Northern General) to the South West (Western National and Devon General), you were never far away from the familiar colours of either red or green and an NBC bus stop. The white paper proposed that the NBC be sold off into private hands and in this way competition would be maximised and fares would be lowered – all to the benefit of passengers.

The white paper quickly became the Transport Act 1985 on 30 October that year and the NBC was directed to draw together a plan on how it might be sold off as quickly as possible while maximising opportunities for competition. The first plan proposed by NBC involved dividing itself into only a few parts. This was flatly refused, with Ridley going further to indicate that he expected some of the largest NBC operations to be split before sale. The second plan offered by NBC suggested breaking up some of its medium-sized operations, namely Bristol Omnibuses, Southdown, United Counties and Alder Valley. Of the largest four operations, only United Automobile was offered up to be split.

United's area of operation was vast with bus depots from Berwick upon Tweed, Wooler and Alnwick in the north to Ripon, Pickering and Scarborough in the south. The fact that United Automobile was offered in the second plan was of particular interest to two senior managers in the company. David Monaghan had started with Sunderland & District in 1953 and since 1976 had been United's Company Secretary, while Tony Kennan was United's Traffic Manager having started with East Kent as a trainee in 1970. Kennan was previously United's Development Officer and had implemented significant changes in the Scarborough area, which had made it a profitable depot within the United operation. Kennan and Monaghan therefore set their sights on obtaining the Scarborough subdivision of United at privatisation.

The second NBC plan was sent to Nicholas Ridley and was again firmly rejected. In his written response to the NBC, on 13 February 1986, Ridley made it explicitly clear that NBC was instead to break up the largest operations, namely United Automobile, Ribble, Crosville and London Country. His letter also stipulated that the Scarborough operations of United should be transferred to the neighbouring NBC operation of East Yorkshire to make the latter more attractive to potential buyers. This was a bitter blow to Monaghan and Kennan as their chance to acquire Scarborough was dashed.

The third and final plan submitted by NBC included the break-up of the largest operations with United Automobile now to be split into three parts – Scarborough to East Yorkshire, and the remainder to be split either side of the River Tyne. Monaghan applied to become Managing Director of operations north of the Tyne and soon learned he had been successful in obtaining what was then known as United North. Kennan soon followed to United North as Commercial Manager and shortly afterwards he noticed, purely by chance, an NBC staff car parked beside his home near Darlington as new neighbours moved in. The car owner was John Fickling, Chief Engineer at East Midland Buses, visiting his brother-in-law. Fickling and Kennan knew each other well having been at Northern General together in the early 1970s and both having been part of NBC's senior management training programme. Conversation soon turned to the radical shake-up occurring within NBC and where everyone was to end up. Fickling was, as a result, soon recruited as United North's Chief Engineer.

As United North's operations would include a considerable amount of running into the Tyne & Wear Passenger Transport Executive (PTE) area, it was felt that having someone with experience of the PTE and local authorities would be advantageous. David Simon had been Group Financial Officer for the PTE since 1976; he and David Monaghan knew each other well and soon Simon had become United North's Finance Director, completing the four top management posts in the new company.

The new team agreed that they wanted a clean break from the NBC and United, with a new identity and approach. Conventional and staid were to be replaced with fresh, vibrant and most importantly different. From around this time in April 1986 United buses operating in Northumberland ceased to be repainted in the previous red fleet livery and were instead turned out in plain white in anticipation of a new livery. As United North were being split off, NBC made money available to the company to fund development of a new identity. Five design houses were offered by NBC to the United North team and one leapt off the page immediately. Hyphen Hayden in London were new and looked best placed to provide the required change of image. Nigel Ferrier with his recently recruited designer Bruce Hugman of Hyphen Hayden met with United North's team in May 1986 and quickly got to grips with the concept of being radical, but with the stipulation made by Tony Kennan that red must still feature on the front of the bus to give reassurance that the buses were still recognisable. The design brief was to include not only a bus livery but a coach livery, publicity, timetables, uniforms and a staff newspaper.

Hyphen Hayden set to work and by June 1986 the company name of Northumbria Motor Services had been agreed (with buses to carry the abbreviated NORTHUMBRIA fleet name). Two design options for a livery then followed in July 1986. Option 1 was a predominantly light grey livery with red skirt and broad red upsweep across the front of the bus. On double-deckers a large area of white covered the front half of the roof and most of the interdeck area. Fleet name was in ITC Eras capitals. Option 2 was a predominantly red bus with a bold dark blue front nearside corner bordered by light grey upsweeps using a kerned variant of Times New Roman font for the fleet name. Both designs were very bold and both broke with tradition by using diagonals and largely ignoring the existing horizontal and vertical seam lines on the bus design, but both had the requested red colour retaining the link to what had gone before. Option 1 was preferred and this became the standard Northumbria livery largely unchanged over the next twelve years.

Northumbria was to formally take over operations from United on Sunday 7 September 1986, and so attention now switched to how best to launch the new company. A bold livery

A choice of two alternate liveries was offered to Northumbria by Hyphen Hayden. Both included diagonals while retaining a degree of red on the front. The upper livery (option 2 described above) eventually became that used by North Western. (David Cook)

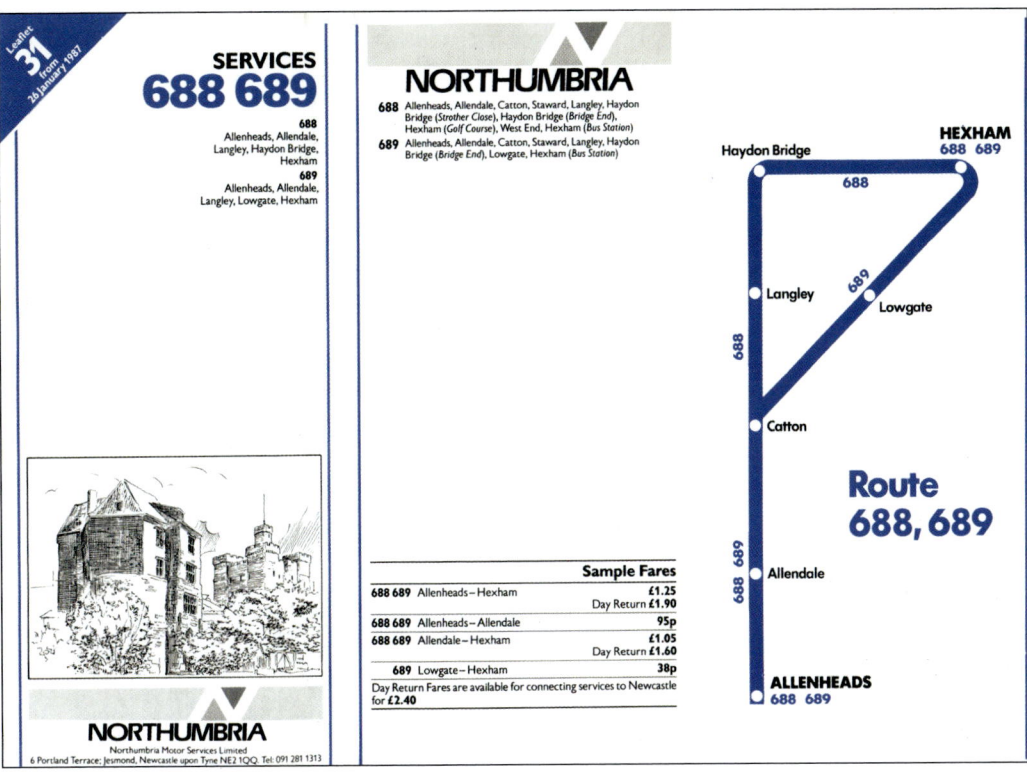

SERVICES

688 689

688
Allenheads, Allendale, Langley, Haydon Bridge, Hexham

689
Allenheads, Allendale, Langley, Lowgate, Hexham

NORTHUMBRIA

688 Allenheads, Allendale, Catton, Staward, Langley, Haydon Bridge (*Strother Close*), Haydon Bridge (*Bridge End*), Hexham (*Golf Course*), West End, Hexham (*Bus Station*)
689 Allenheads, Allendale, Catton, Staward, Langley, Haydon Bridge (*Bridge End*), Lowgate, Hexham (*Bus Station*)

HEXHAM
688 689

Haydon Bridge

688

Langley 689 Lowgate

688

Catton

Route 688, 689

Allendale

688 689

Sample Fares		
688 689 Allenheads – Hexham		£1.25
		Day Return £1.90
688 689 Allenheads – Allendale		95p
688 689 Allendale – Hexham		£1.05
		Day Return £1.60
689 Lowgate – Hexham		38p
Day Return Fares are available for connecting services to Newcastle for £2.40		

ALLENHEADS
688 689

NORTHUMBRIA
Northumbria Motor Services Limited
6 Portland Terrace; Jesmond, Newcastle upon Tyne NE2 1QQ. Tel: 091 281 1313

Hyphen Hayden also designed timetables for Northumbria with clear route mapping, sample fares and a local image on the front cover. (Tony Kennan collection)

needs a bold launch, but it had to be a surprise too; there would be no point in revealing a bus livery that many people had already seen. The centre of Newcastle was the obvious choice but getting a new liveried bus there for the launch without the surprise being spoiled would be extremely difficult. The company also needed promotional materials ready for the launch day. With already painted buses photographed, the first edition of the new staff newspaper – the *Northumbria Herald* – was also to arrive on the same day, revealing the livery to Northumbria staff across the operating area. John Fickling came to the rescue by arranging for the first buses to be painted by his previous employer East Midlands at their central works in Chesterfield. Three vehicles were selected – nearly new Leyland Olympian C264 XEF, along with Leyland National 2 APT 124W and Leyland Leopard coach NDC 504W. The first two were already in plain white for the reason mentioned earlier. The three were dispatched to Chesterfield in August 1986 and were soon outshopped in the new livery. Tony Kennan and John Fickling took their families to Chesterfield to see the buses and while there the vehicles were taken out into the Peak District National Park where the first publicity shots were taken with the two families acting as passengers and the buses screened for far-off destinations such as Newcastle, Whitley Bay and Berwick.

Launch day was set for Thursday 4 September, publicity shots had been done, leaflets prepared, and the first copies of the *Northumbria Herald* were ready to post out. The three repainted buses were moved from Chesterfield to Newcastle under cover of darkness on the night of Sunday 31 August and hidden away in the back of Jesmond depot. After a thorough clean and polish, Olympian C264 XEF was chosen as the launch vehicle and moved out of Jesmond in the early hours of Wednesday 3 September. Commuters heading into Newcastle later that morning may have been somewhat surprised to find a large white box with huge blue bow standing directly in front of the Civic Centre. A gift had been wrapped and given to the city and it was to be unveiled the next day. Two security guards stood watch to make sure the present was not tampered with. Launch day arrived and local comedian Little Billy Fane was hoisted 40 feet into the air by a Newcastle City Council crane. After a last-minute technical hitch caused by a Civic Centre porter turning off the event sound system so he could plug in his kettle, Little Billy pulled the covers off the gift to reveal the first Northumbria bus to the assembled crowd of 300 or so, followed by a ribbon cutting by Newcastle Deputy Lord Mayor Stan Allan.

While the gift was being unwrapped at the Civic Centre the other two repainted buses were brought from Jesmond to the city centre and soon all three moved to Haymarket bus station, where the Olympian took up service on the 16.45 X18 departure to Alnwick on Thursday 4 September – the first bus to operate in service in Northumbria livery, albeit three days before Northumbria services actually started.

Leyland Olympian C264 XEF was wrapped in a blue bow outside Newcastle Civic Centre before the grand livery launch. (Brian Taylor)

AN INTRODUCTION TO NORTHUMBRIA

There is now a major new force in public transport — Northumbria Motor Services Ltd.

Operating a fleet of over 250 buses, all bearing a distinctive grey, red and white livery, Northumbria is set to become the first name in local transport.

The first three buses were repainted in secret at Chesterfield with publicity shots being taken in the Peak District National Park, where Leyland Olympian C264 XEF is seen. (Tony Kennan collection)

With the launch successfully completed, the task of applying new fleet names, legal lettering and operator's discs to the entire fleet was now the focus. Over the weekend of 6–7 September, every bus had its UNITED fleet names covered over by a new NORTHUMBRIA sticker, new discs and legal lettering fitted and, in an extra nod to the new identity, every bus wheel was painted red. This huge job was achieved successfully

Northumbria's opening fleet was made up entirely of buses transferred from United. Typifying the plain image Northumbria were keen to break away from is United's Willowbrook-bodied Leyland Leopard 6228 (AGR 228W, later Northumbria 217), seen between Alnwick and Lesbury in 1983. (Author's collection)

The contrast between Northumbria's stylish new livery and the old NBC United red and white livery is clear here with 6260 (NDC 504W, later 232), one of the three launch vehicles (distinguished by their black grille), leaving Morpeth bus station. (John Carter)

with only the occasional mistake, such as the Redcar bus that had worked to Haymarket on an X16 Sunday service and spent the afternoon layover at Newcastle, during which it was adorned with Northumbria stickers and red wheels. It caused quite a stir when it returned to Teesside that evening.

2

EARLY DAYS: 1986–1987

Northumbria Motor Services began operations on Sunday 7 September 1986 using a licence for the dormant NBC Southern National Omnibus Company. It is important to remember that neither deregulation nor privatisation had occurred at this point and so this was simply a new name for those bus services, buses, staff and depots north of the Tyne formerly operated by United, and still under the ownership of the NBC.

On the first day of operations only local bus services and their buses were transferred. A disagreement had taken place between United management and the new team at Northumbria over how National Express work should be distributed. United felt all the local National Express coaching work should remain with them at the split, whereas Northumbria argued that as Gallowgate depot now fell within their control that any work previously operated from there should be moved to the new company. An impasse was reached and eventually NBC management had to intervene to resolve the issue, with the result being that Gallowgate coaching work would pass from United to Northumbria. This final decision came very late in the preparations for the new company and meant that the National Express coaches and services were transferred to Northumbria around two weeks later than the service bus fleet.

Other than the Northumbria stickers and red wheels, Bristol LH 1655 (LGR 655P, later 615) is little changed from United days during a driver changeover in Blyth bus station. Note the large NBC logo on the driver's equipment box. (Author's collection)

The oldest bus inherited from United was 1971 Bristol RESL 2853 (JHN 553K). Nominally allocated to Wooler, it is seen at Morpeth in 1986 having worked from Bamburgh via Alnwick and Shilbottle. (Author's collection)

Northumberland was a difficult county in which to operate buses. With a very low population density (0.6 persons per hectare) compared to the national average (3.25 persons per hectare) and much of that population concentrated into the south-east of the county in towns such as Ashington, Blyth and Cramlington, much of the network was therefore very rural in nature. Deregulation day for local bus services was only seven weeks away and a possible influx of independent operators onto local services, along with potential competition from larger bus company neighbours. Of the latter there were many: Northumbria had a large operating area meeting NBC subsidiary Cumberland and Scottish Bus Group (SBG – the name for nationally owned bus companies in Scotland) subsidiary Western Scottish in the west at Carlisle; SBG subsidiary Lowland Scottish in the north at Berwick; and NBC subsidiaries United and Northern in the south at Newcastle, along with Newcastle's own large PTE bus fleet. Northumbria viewed the issue of deregulation in reverse. Namely, if independent operators were allowed to begin operating local bus services which they previously largely had not been allowed to do, what aspects of traditionally independent bus operations could Northumbria begin work in? Private hire coaching and contracts (schools and works) were obvious targets and so an active programme of bidding for contracts was begun. Indeed this had already begun before the company was even launched as Borders Regional Council contracts came up for renewal in August 1986. Northumbria bid for these and was successful in winning a number including Berwick to the Scottish town of Duns, the wins coming at the expense of Lowland Scottish. Other operators beyond what had been Northumbria's traditional boundary of operations would soon find the new company prepared to compete for work

Service 447 was one of four services linking Blyth to Morpeth in 1986 and operated via Guide Post. Arriving at Morpeth is Blyth's Bristol VR 694 (UGR 694R, later 515), being followed by reliveried Leyland Leopard 6238 (NDC 238W, later 223). (Author's collection)

Sister Bristol VR 693 (UGR 693R, later 514) shows again the vibrancy of the new livery as it prepares to leave Whitley Bay bus station for Four Lane Ends Metro via Monkseaton and Shiremoor in October 1986. Note the combination of United fleet number and Northumbria livery and the interdeck branding, which would quickly be replaced by advertising. (Author's collection)

The new livery cleverly didn't have any of the colours touching each other to allow simultaneous application. Bristol VR 688 (SUP 688R, later 509) at Ashington proves the livery was just as striking to the rear. (John Sinclair)

Some Berwick vehicles appeared missing fleet names and logos in 1986, including Plaxton-bodied Leyland Leopard 6211 (LGR 411T, later 208). Alnwick's old bus station, seen here, lasted only a few weeks under Northumbria before complete redevelopment and reorientation. (Geoff Stainthorpe)

in South Tyneside, County Durham and Scotland. A coaching unit for private hire work was a high priority and so adverts were quickly placed for a Coaching Manager, while at the same time individual depots were encouraged to promote private hire work using dual-purpose vehicles already in the fleet.

As deregulation approached Northumbria had to decide which services it wished to continue operating commercially, with the remainder passing back to either Northumberland County Council (NCC) or Tyne & Wear PTE to decide whether they wished to put out tenders for their operation. To allow NCC and the PTE sufficient time to carry out the tendering exercise the commercial decisions around routes were actually taken many months earlier in the very earliest days for the new management team. Northumbria registered 79 per cent of its mileage in Northumberland as commercial (but only around 50 per cent of rural mileage) and 68 per cent in Tyne & Wear. NCC did not have sufficient budget to cover the entire shortfall of services and so after a prioritising exercise only some of the work was put out to tender, with Northumbria only winning back 16 per cent of this. The effect on rural bus services was to move previously daily services to only once or twice weekly, somewhat contrary to the stated aims of deregulation of encouraging rural services. In urban areas a policy of making maximum use of buses between the peak hours on weekdays saw NCC having to offer evening and Sunday services out as tenders. In Tyne & Wear the PTE attempted to maintain the full former network and so all the non-commercial work was put out to tender, with Northumbria winning most of its old work back along with a new service – the 9 from Newcastle Central station to Kenton Bar Estate in the north-west of the city.

Deregulation day (D-Day) was Sunday 26 October 1986. Northumbria had lost work in rural Northumberland but offset this with gains in the Scottish Borders. In urban Northumberland some key losses had taken place with independent operator Target Taxis of Cramlington having taken the 417 Morpeth–Lancaster Park; 430 Ashington–North Seaton Colliery; 444 Ashington–Bedlington via Cambois; and the 830 Ashington–Pegswood services, as well as commercially registering two services in Morpeth. The only compensation being that Northumbria had won the tendered parts of service 419 from Morpeth to Scots Gap and Cambo from independent operator T. B. Vasey of Otterburn. The overall changes meant a reduction in requirement for both buses and staff, and it is a sad fact to report that seventy-five drivers were made redundant on deregulation day.

The inherited fleet was giving Northumbria's new Chief Engineer John Fickling much to think about. Fickling had come to his new role after time spent at Northern, Western National, United, South Wales, Yorkshire Traction and East Midland. Of these, Northern, South Wales and Yorkshire Traction had eschewed the more traditional NBC buying policies of Gardner-engined Bristol buses, instead favouring Leyland chassis. Where Bristols were to be purchased, these were usually specified with Leyland engines. Northumbria's fleet included a large number of buses with Gardner engines, bodywork problems were rife, passengers disliked the rough Bristol LH single-deck buses and drivers disliked the poor riding qualities of the Bristol VR double-deckers. The answer was clear to Fickling: Leyland's integral National single-deck bus had some fundamental engine weaknesses but otherwise was a simple, rigid, reliable vehicle that could be standardised upon. The policy was enacted quickly. Even before deregulation the four oldest Bristol VR buses (YHN 654M and BHN 761-3N) were sent to Ribble in exchange for five

Older Bristols were found to be in poor condition and the shortest lived were four Bristol VR/SL2, including 661 (BHN 761N). They lasted only one month before sale to Ribble. (Author's collection)

Northumbria's seven Bristol REs were withdrawn after two months in November 1986. Wooler's RELH 6070 (SHN 70L) leaves Morpeth for Coldstream, a daily service which like many others in rural Northumberland was cut heavily at deregulation. (John Carter)

Leyland Nationals (NTC 634-6/8/9M) that were given temporary fleet numbers 3694-6/7/8. Reduction in vehicle requirement at deregulation gave another opportunity to remove some non-standard vehicles. Two Plaxton-bodied Leyland Leopards (6060/2 – GGR 404/6N) were withdrawn as they were not fitted with power steering (the latter was later converted for use as Jesmond's tow vehicle). Bristol RE single-decks once had been used in vast numbers by United and were well liked by drivers and passengers alike, but Northumbria only received seven of these – six long dual-purpose examples and one short bus. The REs were scattered across the operating area and were now elderly. Gallowgate had 6065 (SHN 65L), Whitley Bay 6075 (SHN 75L), Berwick 6084 (VHN 784M), Ashington 6090 (BHN 690N) and Alnwick 6092 (BHN 692N), while Wooler had two – 6070 (SHN 70L) and the lone short example 2853 (JHN 553K), which was also the oldest service bus transferred to Northumbria. All seven were withdrawn on deregulation day and parked at Hexham depot before being sold to a dealer in February 1987, most moving on to Delta coaches in Stockton-on-Tees for further service. The final cuts were made in the oldest Bristol LHs, where nineteen of the thirty-eight operated were moved to a tactical reserve.

The need to replace the Bristol LH more widely across NBC had led to an agreement to take on a long-term demonstrator from Hestair-Dennis of a Dennis Lancet. The demonstrator had a new 160 bhp Cummins 5.9-litre B series engine and ZF automatic gearbox with Taperlite springs for improved comfort. NBC decided the bus would be sent

Several inherited vehicles initially carried Tyne & Wear PTE livery having previously been used on services exclusively on Tyneside. Bristol LH 1675 (NGR 675P, later 621) shows the PTE yellow colours but now with jarring red wheels as it passes Bedlington. (Author's collection)

Morpeth's new Presto supermarket takes shape in 1986 as Ashington's Leyland National 3108 (RUP 308V, later 774) arrives from Newbiggin and Ashington. Deregulation saw the service 432 via North Seaton Estate disappear as four services were combined into the 335/435. (Author's collection)

The entire fleet was renumbered in November 1986, with those vehicles still in either United red or Tyne & Wear PTE yellow gaining an additional number sticker on the front, such as here on Bristol VR 573 (XPT 798V). (Author's collection)

Bristol LH 615 (LGR 655P) survived the cull of early vehicles which saw fourteen early LHs sold. It is leaving Hexham on an X85 express service for Newcastle, a working which it will struggle to complete in the 42-minute booked time. (Author's collection)

to Northumbria and D631 BPL was duly allocated to Alnwick depot for evaluation after exhibition at the 1986 Commercial Motor Show and given fleet number 650 in anticipation of a new fleet numbering series to be introduced later.

After the delayed transfer of coaching to Northumbria the company had been passed six Bova Europa and two Bova Futura coaches, four Plaxton Paramount-bodied Leyland Tigers, seven MCW Metroliner double-decker coaches and eight Plaxton-bodied Leyland Leopard coaches, all in either National Express or National Holidays livery. The oldest four Leopards (1006/7/14/5 – BBR 996/7S and JUP 114/5T) were immediately repainted into Northumbria livery and downgraded to local service work at Alnwick, Berwick and Morpeth, where their quirky alternating orange and blue reclining seats improved journey comfort on the long 505 service between Berwick and Newcastle. Northumbria had managed to hold on to the prestigious 525 Newcastle, Ashington, Blyth and Whitley Bay to London National Express service as well as routes from Newcastle to Reading, Gatwick and Luton. The 525 immediately came under pressure both from Tyne & Wear PTE's own coaching unit Armstrong Galley, who launched their competing Clipper service, and British Rail who were in the process of electrifying the rail line from King's Cross to Newcastle and beyond at the time. The pressure was resisted and the 525 was retained throughout Northumbria's existence.

Two former Western National Bristol LHs in the Northumbria fleet benefitted from Plaxton coach seats, considerably improving the passenger experience. One of the pair, 632 (VDV 129S), is seen approaching Middleton on the Cambo service. (Bill Counter)

Efforts to find a Bristol LH replacement led to Dennis Lancet demonstrator 650 (D631 BPL) being trialled between 1986 and 1988. It is seen passing Craster harbour on the 501, a typically varied route of narrow country roads and fast dual carriageway. (David Beilby)

Only two distinctive Bova Futura coaches were inherited from United but many more soon followed. One of the original pair, 110 (B210 PDC), is seen in London Victoria while still in National Express livery on the 525 service to Newcastle. (Author's collection)

In their haste to apply red wheels and Northumbria stickers to the whole fleet in just one weekend, coupled with late agreement on the split of National Express and National Holidays work, the occasional mistake was made. Here United's Leyland Leopard 1028 (SUP 728V) at Blackpool has been incorrectly claimed! (Author's collection)

As the fleet had been inherited from United it made sense initially to retain their fleet numbers, but this left huge gaps in sequences and was most untidy. So on the night of Sunday 30 November another full fleet exercise was undertaken when the old United four-digit fleet numbers were removed and new Northumbria three-digit numbers in Helvetica font were applied across the fleet. The new numbering system was much more straightforward. Ancillary vehicles were numbered under 100; full coaches from 100; Leyland Leopard coaches on local service work from 200; Leyland Olympian double-deckers (coach-seated) from 300; Leyland Olympian (bus-seated) from 400; Bristol VR from 500; Bristol LH from 600; and Leyland National from 700. A summary of the renumbered fleet is given in Appendix 1.

Late in 1986 the final legacy from NBC arrived. Harry Blundred had been the Managing Director of NBC subsidiary Devon General and he pioneered the use of small buses operating at high frequency. NBC was persuaded of the merits of this scheme and committed to a large order for minibuses for use across the whole of England and Wales. Northumbria was allocated sixty of this order in the form of Freight-Rover Sherpa sixteen-seat buses that were given fleet numbers 901–60. Painted and stored off site at Thornton Brothers premises in Morpeth, the Sherpa's arrival had been a closely guarded secret for commercial reasons until they were revealed in November 1986. About half were immediately put into tactical reserve, releasing fourteen of Bristol LHs 601–19 for disposal, these ending up with new independent Tyne & Wear Omnibus Company who actively sought and won PTE contracts. The five remaining tactical reserve LHs returned to active service (605, 609, 614, 615 and 618). There were no immediate plans for using the Sherpas and so some were offered out on loan to other operators with the final three (958–60) beginning their lives on loan to Hampshire Bus, being registered there as D958–60 EOW rather than the local D901–57 VCN registrations given to the other buses.

By the start of 1987 Northumbria was now around four months old and industrial relations were starting to strain. Deregulation day had passed and as a result of removal of bus priority measures in the city Newcastle was largely gridlocked. Running times had been tightened by Northumbria to improve their competitive offering and this coupled with the gridlock meant many service timetables were considered unachievable by drivers. Also at deregulation drivers at those depots which had previously had PTE exclusive work rotas (predominantly Whitley Bay and Gallowgate) had been moved to a single uniform company pay rate, losing their PTE enhanced driving rate. Morpeth drivers were unhappy with their Bristol VRs, while northern depots felt their buses were in poor condition generally. The arrival of minibuses had been unexpected and the revelation that minibus drivers would be paid on a lower salary scale was not sitting well. Fortunately the new management team were people focussed and willing to go out and listen to grievances and act wherever possible, with the result that industrial action was minimal and short-lived. Timetables were slackened across the board from January 1987 and a commitment to improve the ride quality of Bristol buses was given. The arrival of new uniforms from 27 July 1987 with the distinctive light grey bomber jackets and trousers was generally well received except at Morpeth depot, where red ties were unwelcome. A letter in the *Herald* complained that 'the new livery made the buses look like they'd come out of a circus and now the management want drivers to dress like clowns'. Inclusion of comments such as these in the *Northumbria Herald* were a key to its success. From the outset effective communication with staff was

North Northumberland benefitted from some wonderfully scenic routes. The 501 followed the rugged North Sea coastline for an hour between Alnwick and Bamburgh, diverting only occasionally to serve small villages such as Howick, where Morpeth's Plaxton-bodied Leyland Leopard 231 (NDC 503W) is seen. (David Beilby)

Travelling across the moors from Wooler in the Cheviot Hills to Alnwick was another striking route and Bristol VR 524 (AUP 714S) will have given its passengers unrivalled views. (David Beilby)

seen as essential to ensure the radical changes were successful. Every quarter a copy of the newspaper was posted to every staff member covering all the company news, both good and bad. Depot correspondents were quickly recruited who covered the local stories in their area and the publication was richly illustrated with staff photos. The Northumbria family was becoming firmly established. It is pleasing to note from *Herald* correspondence that despite the transient skirmishes and isolated examples of unhappiness the overall feeling was that the vast majority of staff were proud and excited to be working for such a forward-thinking company who were willing to defy conventionality but also to listen and react to what their staff wanted.

1987 would also see the widespread deployment of the sixty-strong Sherpa minibus fleet. The same commercial model was used for all minibus operations – using hail-and-ride extensively on a small network of just a few routes in each town. Morpeth and Whitley Bay

THERE'S A WARM WELCOME WAITING ON ALL NORTHUMBRIA'S NEW MINIBUSES IN MORPETH FROM JANUARY 26TH

Small is beautiful
Small buses make more sense for short journeys around local areas. Inside the atmosphere is more intimate and welcoming than larger buses. Minibuses find it easy to nip in and out of community areas and offer fast convenient travel.

Comfort and style
Northumbria Minibuses certainly bring comfort and style to every journey. Modern bus seating and well trained drivers mean every journey is a smooth ride to your destination.

Regular, reliable and roomy
The new minibus service will be more regular and for many areas it means a bus service for the first time. Once inside you'll find that although minibuses are small buses there's plenty of room for your shopping and stretching your legs.

Greater access to *your* area
Minibuses are more versatile too. Requiring less road space they can nip in and out of areas other buses cannot reach quickly and easily.

Your local friend at the wheel
All our minibus drivers are specially hand picked for their warmth and friendliness. They will spend most of their time on the same route so you can take your time getting to know them and they will want to get to know you.

Pick up and set down anywhere – well nearly
That's the beauty of travelling by Northumbria's new minibuses, on some part of the route they'll pick you up nearly anywhere – just signal. And set you down wherever you want – within reason, of course, and as long as it's safe.

There will be 6 minibuses operating in Morpeth from January 26th. And you'll find a warm welcome on board every one, no matter where you're going.

Study the map and timetable to see which route suits you best. Then take your first trip with Northumbria in minibus style, and feel for yourself the warmth of our welcome which will always bring you in from the cold.

New minibus publicity emphasised the hail-and-ride services, versatility of the buses and friendliness of the drivers. Morpeth and Whitley Bay were first to launch on 26 January 1987. (Tony Kennan collection)

Morpeth initially had two minibus services to Kirkhill and in 1989 the M3 was added to Stobhill via Morpeth railway station. Freight-Rover Sherpa 902 (D902 VCN) is seen leaving the bus station on the M3 with two further Sherpas behind. (Author's collection)

began first on Monday 26 January (routes M1, M2 and buses 901–7 in Morpeth; routes W1, W2, W3 and coach-seated buses 918–30 in Whitley Bay), followed by Berwick on Monday 16 March (routes B1 to B5 and buses 908–15 and 932–8), Cramlington on Monday 29 June (routes C1, C2 and Blyth-based buses 940–9) and finally Ashington & Bedlington on Monday 27 July (routes A1–A4 and buses 951–959). In each case the Monday service start was preceded by a Saturday launch invariably including a parade and free giveaways. The buses then ran in service on the Saturday and Sunday for 10p per journey with all money being donated to a local charity. Target Taxis, who had won work in Ashington and Morpeth, now found their core taxi business under pressure by Northumbria's Cramlington minibuses.

In Berwick the arrival of minibuses on town services coupled with the previous Borders Regional Council tenders won by Northumbria ended any cordiality between it and SBG company Lowland Scottish. Lowland and Northumbria shared a depot in the town, separated only by a partition wall and the antecedents of both companies had previously worked jointly on long-distance services between Edinburgh and Newcastle as well as local services in and around Berwick. Northumbria management felt that the town was not large enough for two big operators and struck first with their minibuses in what turned out to be a very bitter and protracted battle for supremacy with both operators running mirrored services on an unsustainable frequency, Lowland from 20 June 1987 using minibuses of their own under the Berwick Beaver brand name.

Minibus operations were launched in Berwick on 16 March 1987 and soon faced stern competition from Lowland Scottish, who also had a depot in the town's bus station. Northumbria's Sherpa 910 (D910 VCN) is seen here with Lowland's Dodge 751 (D751 DSH) with Berwick Beaver branding. (Mike Street)

An early tender win for Northumbria was service 9 in Newcastle between Central station and Kenton Bar Estate. ECW-bodied Leyland Olympian 416 (CEF 230Y) is seen leaving Grainger Street, one of the twenty-one such buses sent to Kentish Bus at the end of 1990. (Author's collection)

Leyland Nationals were favoured by Northumbria over Gardner-engined vehicles. Ex-United 731 (VPT 947R) is seen in a sea of Nationals at Ashington bus station, while former Midland Red 713 (GOL 400N) is alongside. (Author's collection)

Sundays-only service 460 linked Newcastle and Whitley Bay with Cowpen shops in Blyth during the summer of 1990. Gardner-engined Leyland National 2 784 (A133 FDC) is seen at Seaton Sluice. (Author's collection)

Second-hand Leyland Nationals came from many sources including Kentish Bus, Ribble, South Wales and, as here, Midland Red (North). 715 (GOL 404N) is prepared for use in Jesmond depot in May 1987. (Author's collection)

Eight Daimler Fleetlines with Northern Counties bodywork were acquired from Greater Manchester PTE in 1987 and proved very reliable. 598 (OBN 505R) is at Four Lane Ends interchange on the 355 Newcastle–Palmersville circular, while behind Newcastle Busways Leyland Atlantean AVK 171V is heading to Newcastle from Killingworth. (Author's collection)

The vast minibus operation required over forty drivers to be recruited. At about this time many local collieries were closing and a contract with British Coal to retrain redundant miners as bus drivers was negotiated. More driving instructors were recruited and the training fleet was strengthened by the arrival of three more driver trainers – 73 GJG 737D, a 1966 East Kent AEC Regent V; 74 PTF 409G, a 1969 Darwen Corporation Leyland Titan PD2; and 75 CHB 409D, a 1966 Merthyr Tydfil Leyland Titan PD3.

Bodywork on the company's Leyland Leopard coaches was now giving serious cause for concern. The thirteen Willowbrook-bodied examples were only five to seven years old but corrosion issues were obvious and most were temporarily stood down by the end of 1987 while an assessment of their future was made. Of highest priority though were the five Duple-bodied examples, 203–207, where the bodies were described as rotten. The solution came by transferring National Holidays Leopards 123–127 into the service bus fleet, renumbered as 234–237 (PUP 624T, PPT 823T, SUP 326/727V), which allowed the rotten Duples to be withdrawn and sent back to Duple for rebodying. Other notable fleet changes in this period were the arrival of nine 1976/7 Daimler Fleetline buses from Greater Manchester buses (591–9 PRJ 486/8–90/2/4R, OBN 505R, PTD 639S). These proved to be in excellent condition and served Northumbria very well for many years. Eleven more second-hand Leyland National 1 buses arrived from mid-1987 numbered as 710–20 (JOX 498P, TOF 716S, GOL 399–400/3–5/21/31–3N). The arrivals meant that seven early Bristol VR could be withdrawn by the end of 1987. One Bristol VR was given a new life as 555

Northumbria's training fleet began with just two buses, including ex-Midland General Bristol FLF 71 (JNU 989D) on Sea Road, South Shields. The training livery demonstrated how different the new livery would have been without the diagonal lines. (Author's collection)

A contract to retrain redundant coal miners as bus drivers meant the training fleet soon had to expand. Former Bury Corporation Leyland Titan PD2 76 (FEN 587E) was one of several interesting half-cab double-deckers acquired. (Author's collection)

Five Duple-bodied Leyland Leopards were in very poor condition and were soon sent for rebodying. In original condition, 6207 (CUP 707S, later 207) is at Ashington working service 420 from Alnwick, which in 1986 extended to Bedlington. (Author's collection)

The transformation in the rebodied Leyland Leopards was remarkable. Former 6202 (ABR 866S) returned with a new Duple 320 body as 204 (WSV 566) and was initially allocated to Hexham, with similar 203 for use on the long 685 service seen here leaving Carlisle bus station for Newcastle. (Les Simpson)

(OBR 774T) had its roof removed and began service along the Whitley Bay seafront in the summer of 1987 directly competing against Northern's existing service 333. Repaints continued apace at Gallowgate, aided by the clever livery design where none of the grey touched the red so both colours could be applied simultaneously to a plain white base. on 22 March 1988 bus 568 (SGR 791V) became the final bus to receive the Northumbria livery

Arrival of rebodied Leopards 203 and 204 at Hexham for service 685 allowed other Leopards to be cascaded to secondary services. Willowbrook-bodied 219 (AGR 231W) is still branded for the 685 but is at Allendale Town on service 688 heading for Allenheads at the County Durham boundary. (Bill Counter)

Final bus to be repainted from United livery into Northumbria colours was Bristol VR 568 (SGR 791V) in March 1988. It is seen returning to Thropton from the daily schools service to Netherton. Its blinds are already set for the next morning's early service from Rothbury to Newcastle. (Bill Counter)

Alnwick depot had the shortest journey in the area with the four-minute trip to Chapel Lands. With fifty reclining seats and a radio, former National Express Plaxton-bodied Leyland Leopard 236 (SUP 326V) brings some luxury to the steep climb up Clayport Bank. (David Beilby)

Berwick depot had the only service that varied according to the tides. Plaxton-bodied Leyland Leopard 202 (BBR 997S) is seen crossing the tidal causeway to Holy Island with service 477, which ran twice daily but at ten possible times to coincide with low tide. (Bill Counter)

as the repaint programme was completed eighteen months early. A small ceremony was held at Gallowgate where Little Billy Fane (who had unveiled the first bus on launch day) attended and a poem was placed inside the bus to commemorate the event.

Coaching received its much-vaunted launch in 1987. Joanne Barber had joined Northumbria as the Coaching Sales Manager and a successful programme of day and mini-breaks was introduced. Contract holiday work was actively pursued while individual depots continued to promote private hire work. Hyphen Hayden had tweaked their bus livery to use reflective silver instead of matt grey and Bova Futura coach 112 became the first vehicle to carry the coaching livery in February 1987. MCW Metroliner 160 soon followed and became the flagship company vehicle. The coaching fleet was further strengthened by the purchase of two 1983/4 Plaxton Paramount coaches (DAF 120 and Leyland 133), both of which received the new coach livery.

The final significant event of this period was the second part of the original 1985 Transport Act – the sale of Northumbria from NBC into private ownership. Eleven parties expressed an interest in purchasing Northumbria, but only one bid was received, that for £2.4million from Northumbria's own management team. So, on 21 October 1987 at a special ceremony in London, Northumbria passed out of NBC control. The future of the company was now firmly in the hands of David Monaghan, Tony Kennan, John Fickling and David Simon – the first twelve months had seen enormous changes, industrial relations strained and competition beginning in earnest, but going forwards the team could now enact many of their ambitious plans.

A coaching fleet was introduced from 1987 using a modified version of fleet livery. DAF MB200 120 (WSV 573, formerly XRA 4Y) was an early arrival and is seen jostling with London traffic while working a Blue Chip Travel contract. (Geoffrey Morant)

Left: As well as a day tour and mini-break programme coaching was promoted to business travellers with advertising demonstrating the potential for relaxed business meetings on the move. Engineering Director John Fickling accepts the drink while posing as a passenger. (Tony Kennan collection)

Below: Northumbria's directors are seen in London in 1987 on the occasion of the management buy-out from NBC. John Fickling (far left), David Simon (second left), Tony Kennan (second right) and David Monaghan (far right) are seen with NBC Chairman Rodney Lund (centre) and Northumbria crew Ronnie Alderson, Yvonne Betsford and Jimmy Barnes. (Tony Kennan collection)

The classic Northumbria vehicle image was achieved on a Sunday in 1987 when the A167 was closed for maintenance allowing a Metroliner, Leopard and Olympian to be posed on the bridge with a Sherpa and National passing underneath. This is the rarer 'bonus' shot with a fitter taking Bristol VR 513 (UGR 692R) back to Jesmond depot included. (Tony Kennan collection)

3
HALCYON DAYS: 1988–1990

Most operators have a period where everything seems to be running well. For Northumbria this came in the years following the management buy-out on 21 October 1987. After initial losses of around £1.4 million as 1988 began the Finance Director reported that the company was now making money. The 'one big family' feel of Northumbria was being established – a sports committee had begun in 1987 and football, bowls, snooker, darts, squash and badminton were soon bringing staff from across the company together, while Northumbria began sponsorship of Blyth Spartans football team in 1988. For those non-sports fans there were family fun days and a Bus Driver of the Year competition held at Felton. Bristol VR 528 (BPT 920S) was converted into a publicity and hospitality unit to full National Express Rapide specification during 1988 and made regular appearances at staff and public events, renumbered as 20. In 1990 Northumbria Police formed a charity, 'Aid to Romanian Children', and Northumbria Buses were soon involved. Each year the charity sent a convoy of aid to Brasov and in the first year Sherpa minibus 922 (D922 VCN) made the remarkable ten-day 3,500-mile round trip in a support capacity, leaving Newcastle on 12 May 1990.

In 1988 Bristol VR 528 (BPT 920S) was converted into an exhibition and hospitality unit, being finished to National Express Rapide standard. It toured the region attending shows and events, such as here at Washington Galleries. (Author's collection)

Bus advertising was an important source of revenue for the new company, including all-over adverts. Two examples are seen here in Whitley Bay during 1989 with Bristol VR 574 (XPT 799V – 42nd Street Bar Whitley Bay) following Leyland Olympian 429 (C257 UAJ – Direct Windows). (Author's collection)

In an industry first Northumbria was also talking to its passengers and asking them what they wanted from their buses. The first such day had been held in November 1986, hosted by local TV presenter Kathy Secker, and the second followed in April 1988. These consultation days targeted three main groups of passengers: older and disabled passengers, for whom buses were often still largely inaccessible at the time; and women, who Northumbria realised were the main users of their services but using buses designed mainly by men. The results gained were somewhat surprising and showed how far away from desirable current vehicles were. Shallower entrance steps with coloured stripes on step edges, more space for luggage and buggies, better grab rails and better-positioned bell pushes, side and rear destination equipment, and finally better colours for the interior with high-backed seats and soft finishes to interior surfaces were all suggested. This pioneering work led to Northumbria's Commercial Director Tony Kennan becoming an early influential member of the national Disabled Persons' Transport Advisory Committee (DPTAC), which would lead to legislation changes forcing operators to make buses more accessible. Soon an order was placed with MCW for forty-five Metrorider minibuses, and these began to be delivered from November 1987 as buses 801–45 (E801–45 BTN) and featured many of the improvements suggested at the first consultation day. A few weeks earlier the five rebodied 1977 Leyland Leopards (203–7 ABR 865–7S, CUP 706/7S) had returned from Duple transformed into what to most passengers looked like brand-new vehicles disguised behind private numberplates WSV 565–9. They were the first to feature a striking new deep blue seat moquette, exclusively supplied by Holdsworth and selected in conjunction with livery designers at Hyphen Hayden. The seats were deep and welcoming, there was just one problem – there were too many of them. Forty-nine smaller seats had been replaced by fifty-five larger seats and this gave a cramped feel to the interior, a problem that blighted the group as taller adults found them uncomfortable. Fifty-five seats had been selected to satisfy peak-hour capacity on schools contracts. The new Metrorider minibuses featured high-backed seats in the same blue 'Northumbria moquette' and were warmly received, being a big step forward from the rather basic Sherpa minibuses. To reflect their potential for private hire use, Metroriders 801–10 were fitted with luggage boots and a few based at Jesmond for this purpose.

While preparing their management buy-out bid for Northumbria the directors had been reminded that they were not guaranteed to win the bidding competition and were

Above: Many new Northumbria MCW Metroriders began their lives on loan to other operators. 825 (E825 BTN) was one of four on loan to London Buses subsidiary Harrow Buses in 1988. (Author's collection)

Left: In Glasgow Strathclyde Buses borrowed eighteen Metroriders from Northumbria during June 1988. 817 and 818 (E817/818 BTN) battle with the traffic in the unfamiliar surroundings of Rutherglen Main Street. (George Heaney)

posed the question as to how they would feel working for someone else if they were unsuccessful. A contingency plan might be appropriate, perhaps a bid for a second NBC company? Choices were relatively limited as the privatisation process was well underway by then, but a good target seemed to be one of the recently split former London Country operations. What had become London Country (South East) had recently been renamed Kentish Bus with a new livery designed by Ray Stenning. The first visit by the potential bidders didn't go well; it quickly became apparent that Kentish Bus was losing money and Northumbria's Managing Director, David Monaghan, was heard to utter on arriving at Gravesend depot for the first time that 'If Kent is the Garden of England, then this must be the compost heap!'. The potential for growth though was obvious, so a bid was submitted and on 15 March 1988 the company was purchased from NBC. Northumbria was now part of a group of two companies and the name Proudmutual Group was duly adopted for the overarching entity. With 105 minibuses in the fleet at Northumbria and the pressing need to introduce minibus services at Kentish Bus, the logical solution was to send buses south with 845 (E845 BTN) soon becoming the first of many inter-company transfers between the sister companies. The higher specification of the new Metroriders meant they were more desirable in the hire market too and Northumbria soon had Metrorider minibuses on loan to Strathclyde Buses, London Buses, Strathtay Scottish, Maidstone Boro'line, Jubilee Buses, Bexhill Bus Company, Colchester Transport and Wilts & Dorset. Those few which were left were largely allocated to Berwick to augment Sherpas in the ongoing fierce competition with Lowland Scottish and for use on rural services to Wooler.

In Berwick, Northumbria had good wins in the 1988 Borders Regional Council tenders. This included work on the service 23 to Kelso and meant Northumbria buses were now

The new Metroriders also featured on Northumbria's annual calendar. 810 (E810 BTN) fords the River Till in Etal in this publicity shot. (Tony Kennan collection)

The first ten Metroriders were fitted with luggage boots for use on private hire work as well as local service. A trip to de Keukenhof bulb fields in the Netherlands was, however, remarkable for 804 (E804 BTN). Note the overflow luggage piled on the rear seats! (Frans Angevaare)

Even in the later years of Northumbria, service 419 to Cambo and Scots Gap could be relied upon to use a Morpeth-based Bristol LH. In 1990 623 (NGR 683P) returns via Mitford on the then Wednesdays- and Fridays-only service. (Bill Counter)

reaching Dunbar, Duns, Coldstream, Eyemouth and Kelso daily. Edinburgh was on the destination screens of Northumbria buses based at Berwick and serious consideration was being given to commercially operating a service from Berwick to Galashiels to compete with the Lowland service 60. Lowland were under serious pressure in Berwick with their only consolation being a small win on the 505, which took a Lowland bus to Belford each weekday morning. In Newcastle congestion caused by deregulation was easing after a voluntary code of conduct was agreed between the main city operators to keep non-essential services away from the most gridlocked streets. In a surprise move, during September 1988 Newcastle Busways (the new name for Tyne & Wear PTE Buses) handed back many works and schools contracts in south Tyneside. Northumbria bid for all the

During the summer of 1988 Whitley Bay gained an eighth minibus route, W8 from the Metro station to St Mary's Island. Sherpa 923 (D923 VCN) was lettered for the service and is seen with the famous lighthouse behind. (Author's collection)

Sea front service 333 between North Shields Ferry and Whitley Bay began in 1987 using open-top Bristol VR 555. This was supplemented by ex-Kentish Bus 500 (JPL 110K), a Park Royal-bodied Leyland Atlantean transferred for the summer of 1989. (David Little)

work and was extremely successful, the result taking buses to new destinations including Boldon, Whitburn, Hebburn, Brockley Whins, Jarrow and South Shields. Work for ten more vehicles and eleven additional drivers was the result.

The overall profitability of the company allowed orders to be placed for new large buses. The first to arrive were ten new Leyland Olympian double-deckers with bodywork by Alexanders in Falkirk – 303–12 (F303–12 JTY). These new eighty-seaters were launched on 29 November 1988 at Gosforth Park Hotel and boasted a very impressive specification incorporating much of the passenger consultation outcomes around grab rails, low bell pushes, split entrance step as well as luxury coach seating in the Northumbria moquette. Mechanically the buses had a 220 bhp Cummins L10 engine with a ZF 4 speed automatic

South of the Tyne many works contracts were operated to service the vast Team Valley Trading Estate. Daimler Fleetline 592 (PRJ 486R) arrives at the Metrocentre with service 941. (Author's collection)

Schools and works contracts employed many of Northumbria's older double-deckers on weekdays. Here Bristol VR 536 (CPT 734S) has just left the A1 at Scremerston with the morning schoolbus from Wooler to Berwick via Lowick. (Bill Counter)

box, the latter specified as acceleration was prioritised over top speed. At the same time five ex-Green Line long-wheelbase ECW Coach Leyland Olympians were being transferred from Kentish Bus as 351–5 (A101–5 FPL). The new Olympians were initially split between Blyth (303–7) and Ashington (308–12) depot with the ECW coaches 351–5 also going to Blyth to improve services between those towns and Newcastle. Passengers were extremely impressed, but other operators less so. New 303 was exhibited at the 1988 Commercial Motor Show where it was unkindly nicknamed the Habitat bus (after the furniture store of the same name) due to its resemblance to a modern living room rather than a service bus interior. This unfair nickname now reveals much more about how far ahead of other operators Northumbria was

Brand-new double-deckers came late in 1988 with ten impressive long-wheelbase Alexander-bodied Leyland Olympians. Initially based at Blyth and Ashington for Newcastle services, 310 (F310 JTY) calls at Bedlington heading for Newbiggin. (Author's collection)

New single-deckers soon followed in the shape of Optare Delta-bodied DAF SB220 buses. First of the second batch 255 (G255 UVK) is seen on the 1990 Gateshead Garden Festival shuttles. (Author's collection)

at the time, some of whom took two more decades to reach the same standard of passenger comfort. From January 1989 the first four DAF SB220 single-deck buses were entering service at Jesmond as 251–4 (G251–4 SRG). These forty-eight-seater lightweight construction buses had Optare Delta bodywork again to Northumbria's advanced luxury interior specification. A second batch of four followed in May 1990, 255–8 (G255–8 UVK), and were initially used on Gateshead Garden Festival shuttles before being trialled at Hexham depot on the 685 Newcastle–Carlisle service. The final group of nine arrived in December 1990 as 259–67 (H259 CFT, H598 CNL, H261–7 CFT) and were split between Gallowgate (259–60), Blyth (261–4) and Hexham (265–7). The next ten second-hand ECW Olympian coaches were arriving at the same time, becoming 356–65 (C211–3 UPD, C448–51 BKM, C452–4 GKE) and were allocated to Whitley Bay (356–8) and Hexham (359–65) to improve Tynemouth and Prudhoe services. These arrivals along with more second-hand Leyland Nationals, 721–6 (to suburban coach specification) from Kentish Bus and 736–40 from South Wales late in 1989 and ten further Kentish Bus examples in 1989/90 as 741–50, allowed a large number of Bristol VRs to be disposed of with most of 501–525 having left the fleet by the end of 1990.

The additional work meant even more pressure on the training school and a backlog of drivers waiting for driving tests. More training buses were required and 76 (FEN 587E), a 1967 Bury Corporation Leyland Titan PD2, arrived in December 1987. Trainer 72 was replaced with 77 (MFN 951F), a 1967 East Kent AEC Regent V, in July 1988, while trainers 71 and 75 were replaced by ex-Southdown 1965–6 'Queen Mary' Leyland Titan PD3s

As well as the coaching unit, each depot was encouraged to promote local private hire work with Morpeth being the most successful at this. Proving all vehicles could be used, sixteen-seater Sherpa 902 (D902 VCN) crosses the Pauperhaugh Bridge near Rothbury with a private party. (Bill Counter)

At the other end of the private hire spectrum the seventy-four-seat MCW Metroliner 160 (NMS 700) was Northumbria's flagship coach. It is seen on Edinburgh's Waverley Bridge before returning south. (Alistair Train)

78 and 79 (BUF 277C, FCD 286D) in February 1989, these being the last of the remarkable vintage double-decker training bus fleet to be acquired. In a further example of listening to staff suggestions, it transpired two of the driving instructors were qualified to train HGV (lorries) as well as PCV (buses). As a result, Dodge Commando artic 60 (EVM 368Y) was acquired and training expanded to include HGV lessons.

Coaching was also flourishing, growing at over 200 per cent per year at some points. The in-house travel agency Norham Travel was established and the Ashington travel office was the first to be rebranded. Contract work was secured from Omega Travel and Blue Chip Travel. Additional coaches were needed urgently to meet the demand and so three new and five second-hand Bova Futuras were acquired, becoming 111, 113–9, all carrying private registrations. Two new Plaxton Expressliners 150/1 (G150/1 XFT) and two second-hand MCW Metroliners 192/3 were acquired for National Express work, which allowed some previously dedicated buses to be released to the contract coaching pool. Still with insufficient capacity to meet demand the coaching division was forced to hire coaches from Hughes-DAF in the form of Van Hool-bodied 140-2 (F267 RJX, E633 KCX, D276 XCX) during the summer of 1990.

Advertising was reviewed in this period. Marcel, a mime artist, was revealed in print and TV advertising from 18 April 1989 in an attempt to improve the image of Northumbria among its customers, recent surveys having suggested passengers felt the company was big and anonymous and not sufficiently connected to their local community, and also did not

Training School activities were diversified to include HGV training, and Dodge Commando 60 (EVM 368Y) was acquired. Here the trainee is about to negotiate Newcastle's Haymarket with Leopard 218 (AGR 229W) following on service X1 from Blyth. (Bill Counter)

The final two double-decker training buses arrived from OK Motor Services in 1989. One of a pair of former Southdown 'Queen Mary' Leyland Titan PD3s, 78 (BUF 277C), is seen outside Ashington depot. (The Bus Archive)

Two Duple-bodied Leyland Leopards acted as Proudmutual Group pool vehicles and could be used at any subsidiary with short notice. 652 (SPW 103R) has a rather carelessly applied 'N' on its temporary fleet name at Ashington in 1991. (Author's collection)

In June 1989 it is 15.10 and Bristol VR 519 (UGR 702R) emerges from a sea of competing minibuses at Berwick bus station with the daily service to Dunbar, a mere 30 miles from Edinburgh. Dunbar was the farthest north Northumbria reached on regular service. (Author's collection)

From 1993 Alexander-bodied Leyland Olympians 310-312 moved to Gallowgate depot to improve the offering on service 604 between Newcastle and Prudhoe. 311 (F311 JTY) passes the Co-operative clock on Newgate Street. (Author's collection)

Former Green Line long-wheelbase Leyland Olympian coaches started arriving in 1988 for Tynemouth and Prudhoe services. 362 (C451 BKM) makes for Hexham in 1993 as it leaves Newcastle's Percy Street. (Richard Simons)

stand out from other companies in the area. This was a blow to the team, who redoubled efforts to change this impression. One aspect of the new advertising was called Action in the Community. Every depot in the fleet soon had its own dedicated charity. Northumbria buses appeared at events across the region, often being pulled to raise money. The other side to the advertising was a prize draw whereby customers of participating local businesses including NEEB and Callers-Pegasus could win their spend back by submitting their bill and a Northumbria bus ticket for entry into a weekly draw. There was soon also a Northumbria Bears scheme in which passengers saved bus tickets and could exchange these for gifts at travel shops. This scheme proved to be extremely popular. At events and across the advertising media, Marcel became the distinctive advertising face of Northumbria. Bus advertising too was crucial. In the only significant change to the original livery some buses had bodyside fleet names moved to the space above side windows to allow advertising on side panels to be carried by most vehicles in the fleet. Large numbers of all-over adverts were characteristic of the fleet for most of its existence, the most memorable perhaps being a strident yellow advert for Pennine Windows, which was carried by several vehicles over the years.

Diversification and expansion was also the philosophy elsewhere and from late 1988 Blyth depot were offering car MOTs. Northumbria began Furst Garages in July 1990, a Renault dealership, and had branches established in Scremerston near Berwick (with a new depot door big enough to accommodate double-deckers buses) and Ashington, while in the same year it acquired three car transporters and began moving cars around the country for BCA and ADT auction houses. Nothing seemed off limits and a smoked salmon company was

1989 saw the first use of Marcel the mime artist, who would soon be a regular feature of Northumbria's advertising. Here Marcel is seen filming a TV commercial for the 'bill paid' prize draw. (Tony Kennan collection)

Marcel was soon appearing on the sides of buses throughout the region. Bristol VR 514 (UGR 693R) carries the 'Turn your tickets into cash!' slogan while at Holy Island. (Bill Counter)

even very briefly considered for purchase. The company also acquired a number of local rivals including Moor-Dale Curtis and R&M in December 1989, H. E. Craiggs and Wansbeck in February 1990 and Longstaffs in April 1990. The most significant event was however the long-awaited sell-off of Scottish Bus Group companies, and first to be advertised was Northumbria's nemesis in Berwick, Lowland Scottish. A bid was placed and the company were told they had been successful in acquiring the company. Politics then intervened and the sale was subject to a review in which Northumbria had their bid cancelled. Lowland was instead sold to a management buy-out and the battle for control of Berwick continued.

Losing Lowland was not however the only piece of bad news in this period of otherwise general positivity. Industrial relations were still strained, the *Herald* reporting issues at various times raised by staff at Blyth, Whitley Bay, Cramlington and a work-to-rule by Newcastle staff all blighting relations. All National Holidays contracts were lost in 1988 due to unreliability of vehicles used. A Berwick-based engineer was taken to court in August 1988 after sabotaging the entire depot fleet. Newcastle Busways began a new competitive service, X22, between Cramlington and Newcastle which hit revenue, as did OK Motor Services starting to compete on Prudhoe–Newcastle services. OK also managed to win services 673 Newcastle–Apperley Dene and 687 Horsley–Hexham from Northumbria in April 1988. Buses 759 and 765 were written off in accidents, 162 was severely damaged in a crash on the A1, 751 and 723 were burnt out, 163 caught fire and took over a year to repair, 629 was stolen from Whitley Bay and recovered badly damaged, and 534 was blown off the road in gales, while 828 was written off while on loan to Kentish Bus without ever having

Passenger consultation quickly revealed a preference among passengers for coach-seated vehicles. Despite only inheriting two Leyland Olympians with coach seats from United, Northumbria soon acquired others second-hand and began converting some bus-seated examples. One of the original pair, Morpeth's 301 (C263 XEF), arrives at Newcastle Haymarket on its regular X18 service from Alnwick. (Author's collection)

A short-lived all-over advert was for Canadian Pacific Air Lines on Bristol VR 586 (APT 819W) seen alongside Northumbria's mini van 32 (PDC 782X) in full fleet livery. (Author's collection)

From 1991 all five Duple 320 rebodied Leyland Leopards were concentrated on Alnwick, Berwick and Morpeth depots for use on service 505. Morpeth's 206 (WSV 568, formerly CUP 706S) is seen on a private hire outside Newcastle Central station. (Author's collection)

After their time on National Express work was over five of Northumbria's six Bova Europa coaches were disposed of in 1991, the exception being 108 (OSK 775, formerly B208 NEF), which was retained and repainted into coaching livery. It is seen here on Newmarket Promotions contract work. (Author's collection)

worked for Northumbria. All of these were weathered without too much difficulty, but two events in 1989 were to prove to be of much greater consequence.

In the early hours of Wednesday 28 June 1989 two academically high-flying schoolchildren from Sunderland were in Wooler celebrating the end of their A-levels. By now heavily intoxicated, they decided to take a bus for a drive but being unable to do so they instead set fire to Bristol VR 545 (DUP 752S), which was parked outside the depot. The fire quickly spread out of control into adjacent bus 532 (BPT 926S). Soon one of the tyres on 545 exploded and the burning debris punctured the depot door, where Bristol LH 628 (SNU 385R) and MCW Metrorider 808 (E808 BTN) were soon ablaze. All four buses were burnt out but were it not for the heroic efforts of Wooler lead driver Alan Brown, driving three more Metroriders and a Bristol LH out of the burning depot, the damage could have been worse. As the buses were insured on a new-for-old basis, Brown was jokingly questioned the next day as to why he'd saved the elderly LH! After an offer from Farmway for the site, Wooler depot was eventually sold on 29 June 1990.

Also in 1989, from 28 March, Target Taxis of Cramlington had decided they had had enough of Northumbria minibuses muscling in on their hometown taxi business. They launched the TX1 bus service linking Blyth and Cramlington with Newcastle. Northumbria retaliated on 30 April with their X1 service timed to run at exactly the same time and route as the TX1. Competition was soon intense with the two companies trying to undercut and outperform each other. In October 1989 Northumbria even resorted to repainting Leyland Olympian 433 (C261 UAJ) in plain white in an effort to fool passengers into thinking the bus was a Target-operated vehicle. It was the first of several buses to be treated as such in so-called anti-Target white.

Aftermath of the 1989 Wooler depot arson attack. The remains of Bristol VR 532 (BPT 926S) and 545 (DUP 752S) are seen here with the frame of Bristol LH 628 (SNU 685R) just visible beyond. (John Sinclair)

To aid with the vehicle shortage after the Wooler fire two vehicles were borrowed from Go-Ahead Northern for two weeks. Ashington received Leyland National RPT 754V while Wooler used Bristol LH AHN 611M, seen here with 631 (VDV 125S). (Author's collection)

Target Taxis of Cramlington competed fiercely with Northumbria between 1989 and 1994 on the Blyth–Cramlington–Newcastle corridor. Both operators used white vehicles with red wheels. This Bristol VR/SL2 SHE 818M is a Target Taxis vehicle... (Author's collection)

...while this Leyland National 2 MHN 131W was Northumbria 733, based at Blyth where a dedicated rota of drivers for anti-Target routes was used. Both are seen near Newcastle Haymarket. (Author's collection)

4

RECESSION: 1991–1994

If the years 1987–1990 were the peak for Northumbria, those in the early 1990s would prove to be much more challenging. Most of the reasons for this downturn were external and affected bus operators throughout the country. 1991 saw the economy fall into recession, unemployment climb sharply and the Gulf War caused fuel prices to double. Within Northumbria this meant in real terms growth of 4.4 per cent per year but costs increasing at a rate of 8.7 per cent. In his end-of-year report for 1991, Chairman David Monaghan announced that although a modest profit would be made it would not be enough to allow further new vehicles to be purchased. By 1992 the same year-end message simply described 1992 as 'a terrible year'. The recession ended in 1992 but its effects lingered on well beyond.

A lack of money in customers' pockets meant discretionary purchases suffered particularly. Coaching was badly hit with Northumbria's own tours programme becoming loss-making. Work from contract tour operators was still available and Northumbria had earned a good reputation for this work. Enhanced contractual rates for carrying tour operators' names were enjoyed in this period with several Bova Futura coaches carrying a modified version of Northumbria's coaching livery with blue skirt along with either Omega Holidays or Blue Chip Travel names, but retaining a large Northumbria 'N' on the front and Northumbria antimacassars on the seats. Work from Newmarket Travel and Cotswold Travel was also won. To supplement the coach fleet MCW Metrorider minicoach 101 (HKR 11) was acquired in summer 1992 from recently closed Maidstone Boro'line.

Shortly before the arrival of coach 101 in 1992 Proudmutual Group had been in negotiations to purchase Maidstone Boro'line but failing this, in the end, only the London Transport contracts and the associated vehicles were purchased and transferred to Kentish Bus. This enhanced Kentish Bus' status as one the largest contract providers to London Transport and a financial jewel in the crown for Proudmutual.

Contract wins were also in the news for Northumbria. Having lost almost all of its Scottish contract work in 1990, wins in the Borders Regional Council tenders of 1992 took Northumbria buses back to Eyemouth and Kelso on weekdays. At the opposite end of the region Durham County Council wins in 1991 saw Hexham retaining service 773 and gaining the 763/764.

Above: From 1990 a new livery with blue skirt was introduced in the coaching division for those vehicles dedicated to contract work. One of the first pair treated was Bova Futura 117 (GSU 347 formerly F570 KGX) for Omega Holidays, seen at the National Motor Museum Beaulieu in 1991. (Mike Street)

Left: Another Northumbria calendar image shows MCW Metrorider coach 101 (HKR 11, formerly G298 SKP) on the harbour wall at Seahouses with Bamburgh Castle in the distance. (Tony Kennan collection)

Twenty-one bus-seated Leyland Olympians were transferred to sister company Kentish Bus in 1990/1 for new contract wins. Former 417 (CEF 231Y) is seen in Harmer Street, Gravesend, before taking up a schools service. (Author's collection)

Kentish Bus proved a valuable source of the much-favoured Leyland National with twenty-eight being transferred north. 750 (UPB 315S) arrived in March 1990 and is seen still in Kentish Bus livery leaving Morpeth depot for service to Whitley Bay. (Author's collection)

To aid with withdrawal of life-expired Willowbrook-bodied vehicles, four Leyland Leopards arrived from Kentish Bus in July 1991. Alnwick depot received Duple Dominant-bodied 238 (GDF 277V), outside which it is seen receiving attention in 1995. (Steve Johnson)

For the summer of 1992 six Plaxton Paramount-bodied Leyland Tigers were transferred from Kentish Bus to Hexham depot for Newcastle to Carlisle service 685. 246 (B276 KPF) is seen at Gallowgate on summer Coastlink service 422 from Bridlington while still in Green Line livery and mistakenly numbered 242. (Author's collection)

Winning tendered service 773 took Northumbria to Consett in County Durham five times per day from Townfield and Blanchland. Hexham stalwart Leyland Leopard 209 (LGR 413T) is seen on layover, uniquely retaining its Plaxton Supreme III front end. (Author's collection)

Northumbria also won the five-year Tyne & Wear Carebus contract (to provide accessible transport across Tyne & Wear) from September 1992 and as a result two fully accessible vehicles were required. Leyland National 701 (THX 192S) was acquired from London Buses already converted for use with dual doors, twenty-one seats and a wheelchair lift. From within the Northumbria fleet Leyland National 2 786 (A141 FDC) was sent to East Lancashire Coachbuilders for conversion under their Greenway rebuild programme. It returned as bus 702 (XSV 238) with twenty-three high-back seats and wheelchair lift in a distinctive orange livery usually driven by dedicated driver Brenda Ingham.

Despite the Chairman's warning that no new buses would be arriving soon, the fleet was in remarkably good shape at the start of 1991. 'Habitat' Olympians 303–312, along with what would soon total eighteen luxury ECW Olympian coaches 351–368, and seventeen Optare Delta single-decks 251–267 had transformed journeys between Ashington, Blyth, Whitley Bay, Tynemouth, Hexham, Prudhoe and Newcastle – all with Northumbria's distinctive blue moquette coach seats. Morpeth and Alnwick depots shared coach-seated Olympians 301, 302 and 'Habitat' 307 for the X18 Alnwick to Newcastle via Amble service. Transfer of twenty-one Leyland Olympians with bus seats (410–30) to Kentish Bus early in 1991 to assist with London Transport contract wins allowed a further two coach-seated Olympians, 341–2 (EEH 901/8Y), to come north, 341 supplementing the others at Morpeth on the X18. From late 1991 a further four of the remaining bus-seated Olympians were sent to MTL in Liverpool for full refurbishment and conversion to coach seating, being renumbered from 404-6/8 to 343–6 (SPY 205/10X, WDC 212Y, SPY 204X).

With twenty-five coach seats the MCW Metroriders proved extremely versatile, whether providing extra capacity on town minibus services or, as here, for lightly loaded rural services. 809 (E809 BTN) has reached the top of Lemmington Bank on service 473 between Wooler and Alnwick via Powburn, Glanton and Whittingham. (Bill Counter)

Northumbria were at the forefront of providing accessible transport and it was entirely fitting they should win the Tyne & Wear Carebus contract in 1992. Two Leyland Nationals were used: 786 (A141 FDC) from within the fleet, which was painted bright orange; and 701 (THX 192S), sourced from London Buses specifically for the work and seen loading outside Crowtree Leisure Centre in Sunderland. (Author's collection)

One group of vehicles now in dire need of replacement were the thirteen Willowbrook-bodied Leyland Leopards 215–222, 224–8. Consideration was given to a rebodying programme like that undertaken with 203–7, indeed the bodies of 217 and 219 were removed and scrapped with the chassis being stored in September 1991, but the project did not proceed, the chassis later being scrapped. The solution came from Kentish Bus and displaced Green Line express coaches. Four Leyland Leopards arrived in August 1991 as 238–41 (GDF 277V, SND 296X, YEL 97/8Y) at Alnwick and Morpeth, while a year later in August 1992 six Plaxton Paramount-bodied Leyland Tigers 242–7 (B262/5/73/9/6/7 KPF) were sent to Hexham to upgrade the 685 Carlisle service. By now only four Willowbrooks remained. Other notable fleet changes in his period saw the training fleet replaced in May 1991, all the vintage double-deckers being sold and replaced by four Bristol LHs from within the fleet – 605 (WHN 594M), 614 (LGR 654P), 631 (VDV 125S) and 618 (MGR 659P), which were renumbered 86–9 for the work. A notable event occurred in July 1992 when twelve Leyland National 1 buses were initially loaned and subsequently sold to South Riding Buses in Sheffield. The loan, involving buses 716/7/20/31/2/51-3/61/7/71, turned out to be the beginning of the end for this once ubiquitous bus type in the Northumbria fleet as withdrawals began in earnest soon afterwards.

Charity and staff engagement work continued apace, Northumbria being acutely aware of the pressures its staff and families were under during the recession. Rather than diminish their staff engagement to save money it now seemed more important than ever to maintain and build upon it. Regular inter-group sports weekends saw Kentish and Northumbria teams go head-to-head, while the company's family fun days at Stannington in 1991 and

1992 and Whitley Bay's Spanish City in 1993 saw 2,500 staff and their families attend for a day of fun. Football, darts, dominoes, pool and many other sports saw Northumbria depot teams at every depot playing teams ranging from cub scouts to the likes of Safeway supermarket and Ashington General Hospital all in aid of local charities. At Whitley Bay staff even dressed in frocks to raise money for the RVI Hospital in Newcastle. Further afield work with the Northumbria Police Aid to Romanian Children charity took a big step forward when Blyth depot converted recently withdrawn Willowbrook-bodied Leyland Leopard 215 (TPT 22V) into a mobile dental surgery. It was donated to the charity and driven to Brasov on 15 April 1993 by two Blyth depot engineering staff.

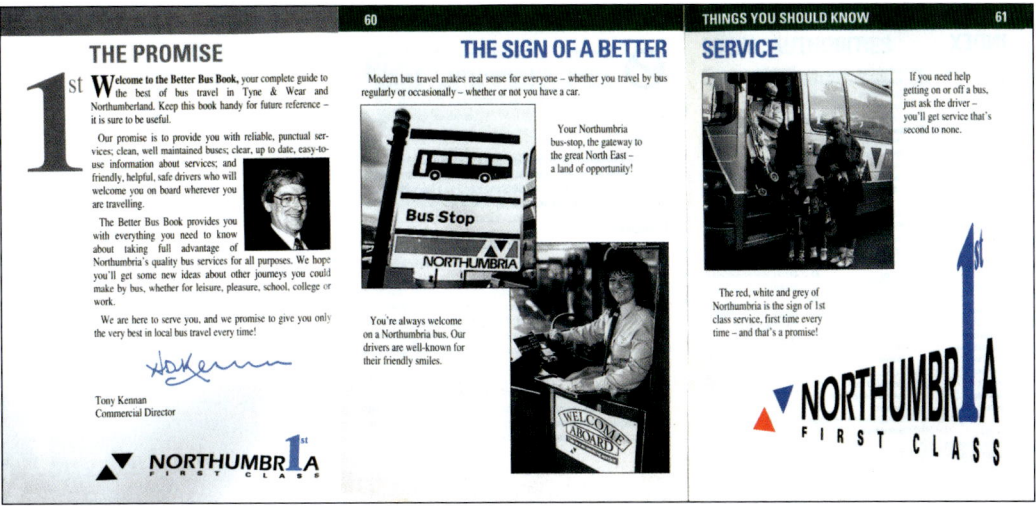

In 1992 the award-winning *Better Bus Book* was published and distributed to all homes in the operating area. The book included a service promise signed by Commercial Director Tony Kennan and sixty-five pages of helpful guidance including how to use buses and where to find help. (Tony Kennan collection)

Training was overhauled in summer 1991 with the elderly double-deckers being replaced by four Bristol LH service buses in a new training livery incorporating a blue skirt. The fleet was based at Ashington depot, where 87 (LGR 654P) is seen. (Author's collection)

Most Willowbrook-bodied Leyland Leopards were withdrawn and disposed of in 1991. 215 (TPT 22V) was reprieved and sent to Blyth depot for full overhaul and conversion to a mobile dental surgery before being donated to the Northumbria Police Aid to Romanian Children charity. It was driven to Brasov in Romania in April 1993 by Northumbria staff, where it remained to serve the local population. (Author's collection)

Twelve Leyland Nationals were loaned and then sold to South Riding Buses in 1992. Whitley Bay's former 767 (JBR 688T) is seen at Woodhouse, south of Sheffield. (Richard Simons)

Northumbria's innovative approach was also becoming recognised nationally and a well-earned Service Delivery award in January 1992 recognised the changes across the company. The team weren't going to rest on their laurels however, and the adoption of a Total Quality Management system in 1991 was soon followed in 1992 by another industry first – the Better Bus Book. This new book explained in simple terms how to use buses, the types of tickets available, a summary of routes at each bus station along with an introduction to the local manager to whom enquiries could be made. A copy was posted to every house in the operating area. Industry awards including a prestigious Plain English Award soon followed. Smoking on buses had proved to be an issue that consultation days had revealed to be unpopular and so from 13 March 1991 a voluntary ban on smoking on buses was introduced, followed on 3 February 1992 by a compulsory ban. A Cramlington woman was soon in court for smoking on a Northumbria bus in a story that achieved national media attention, being the first such case in Britain.

The smoking ban came a little too late for Olympian coach 353 (A103 FPL), which was burnt out on the A1058 Coast Road late in 1990 by a carelessly discarded cigarette. After eighteen months it returned to service with a new Northern Counties Palatine 1 coach body and soon became a test bed for the new Gardner LG1200 engine. Re-engining existing fleet vehicles was trialled extensively in this period as Leyland Nationals 736/7 were fitted with Volvo and 730/787 with Cummins engines, Leopards 204/7 gained Leyland TL11 engines, and Olympian 360 a Cummins L10, while 314 received a further Gardner LG1200 engine. Refurbishment of the MCW Metroriders (801–45) and earlier Optare Deltas (251–8) was now also necessary to bring them up to DPTAC standard, particularly the replacement of small dot matrix displays on both bus types as well as new interior fitments for the Metroriders.

In March 1991 Northumbria were delighted to learn that long-term competitor Target Taxis had had their licence to operate revoked, but irritatingly the operator was soon back with service TX1 under sister Crown Coaches licence. Competition was again fierce with Target and Northumbria operating near identical services on routes X1/TX1 and X23/TX23 between Blyth and Newcastle. A fleet of white anti-Target Leyland National 2 buses (733–5) and a dedicated rota of drivers was soon in place at Blyth. Competition finally ended early in 1994 when Target withdrew.

March 1991 also saw the launch of service M64, branded as the Riverside Express. It linked Eldon Square and Central station with the new Riverside Business Park at Elswick. The service was immediately very popular and loadings increased even more when route-dedicated coach-seated Leyland Nationals 721/2/4 (WPG 217M, XPD 233N, GPD 296N) replaced Sherpa minibuses in March 1992. The M64 was described as the success story of 1992, but the business park expanded so rapidly that it was soon necessary to divert all passing services into the park. In June 1993 service A5 began between the old Ashington General Hospital and its newly opened replacement, Wansbeck General Hospital. The service was very unusual, not just because it ran every day of the year but also because the three dedicated MCW Metroriders on the route towed a large blue trailer allowing supplies and food to be moved between the two hospitals while services were transferred. Summer 1994 saw a six-week experiment on the north Northumberland coast between Beadnell and Bamburgh with the first use of an open-top bus (555 YCU 961T) in service away from the regular summer 333 Whitley Bay seafront service.

During 1992 several West Midlands Transport MCW Metroriders were borrowed to allow Northumbria's own Metroriders to be upgraded to DPTAC standard. One of the loans was 6370 (D637 NOE), seen at Four Lane Ends on the Palmersville M55 service. (Author's collection)

After refurbishment Northumbria's Metroriders featured larger roller blind destination screens as well as several internal accessibility changes. 836 (E836 BTN) in Ashington is working hospital service A5, which operated every day of the year and towed a supplies trailer. (John Carter)

In 1993 former London Transport Bristol LH 628 (OJD 95R) was acquired specifically to operate Alnwick town service 472, for which it had fixed blinds. It is seen in Windsor Gardens during September 1995. (Steve Johnson)

Service 306 was a 40-minute journey from Newcastle to Tynemouth along the Coast Road operating every 15 minutes. Last of the eighteen Leyland Olympian coaches was 368 (B697 BPU), acquired from Eastern National in 1992 and seen outside Tynemouth Priory. (Author's collection)

Leyland Olympian coach 353 (A103 FPL) was burnt out while working a service 306 in 1990. The chassis was sent to Northern Counties for rebodying, returning in 1992 to resume service re-registered OSK 774 and with an evaluation Gardner LG1200 engine. (Author's collection)

In 1991 new service M64 was launched linking Newcastle with the Riverside Business Park in Elswick. It soon proved so popular that the original minibuses had to be quickly replaced by route-branded Leyland Nationals. Peugeot-Talbot Pullman demonstrator H163 EFK is seen on the service in July 1991. (Author's collection)

Leyland National 787 (NPK 253R) was experimentally fitted with a Cummins engine, which involved removing some of the rear seating. This April 1995 view in Ashington shows the extent of the rear bodywork modifications required. (Steve Johnson)

Northumbria were prolific users of manufacturer demonstrator vehicles with many types large and small being trialled over the years. Robin Hood-bodied Iveco 49.10 F368 RPO is on trial during May 1989, passing West Monkseaton Metro on service W3. (Author's collection)

After spending most summers on the Whitley Bay seafront service, Bristol VR 555 (YCU 961T, formerly OBR 774T) was trialled between Bamburgh and Beadnell during 1994. Sale of the company to British Bus later that year saw both open-top buses quickly sold. (Author's collection)

7 March 1994 saw the introduction of National Express Rapide Plus specification on the Newcastle–London corridor. The service standard that had been conceived by Tony Kennan was launched with three new Bovas 136–8 (L766–8 YTN) along with converted and renumbered 134 (NMS 700), previously flagship coach 112. Rapide Plus included a check-in facility and first-class standard waiting room at Gallowgate along with a covered departure stance. Other fleet Bovas were progressively upgraded to the new specification and renumbered into the 130 series, but this sadly meant the end for the impressive MCW Metroliner double-decker coaches and on 6 March 1994 former flagship coach 160 made the last trip to London for the type.

It had been an undeniably difficult period. Within the company, plans to expand Furst Garages into Morpeth using a combined site with a new bus depot on Coopies Lane were thwarted, an arson attack at Blyth depot on 10 April 1993 destroyed Bristol VRs 571 (SGR 796V), 582 (APT 815W) and National 719 (GOL 432N) and severely damaged National 2 734 (RDC 735X). These were closely followed by very disappointing results in the 1993 north Northumberland tenders, Alnwick depot and Wooler outstation being the worst affected with seven drivers, two fitters and four cleaners losing their jobs as a result. But as before the worst news came from an external source as 1,100 people lost their jobs in February 1994 when Ellington Colliery near Ashington was closed. The recession may have been over but continuing to provide a quality service in an area with soaring unemployment was not going to be easy.

Introduction of Rapide Plus by Northumbria in 1994 meant London-bound services at Gallowgate had their own first-class waiting area, check-in and undercover boarding stance. Bova Futura 136 (WSV 570, formerly L766 YTN) is seen in the boarding bay ready to work the next London-bound service 525. (Steve Johnson)

The introduction of Rapide Plus in 1994 meant the end for Northumbria's fleet of MCW Metroliners. 159 (B337 WFJ) was one of the last four and is seen leaving London bound for Darlington. (Author's collection)

Somewhat surprising purchases in 1992 were three sixteen-year-old Leyland Atlanteans from Newcastle Busways with that operator's distinctive nearside staircase layout. 503 (MVK 522R) is at Front Street Dinnington on the frequent service 45 from Newcastle Haymarket. (Author's collection)

Leyland National 2 780 (APT 127W) spent almost its entire working life at Ashington depot. Here in 1996 in its final year it leaves Morpeth bus station once again for Newbiggin. (Steve Johnson)

5
NEW OWNERS: 1994–1998

The news that Northumbria Motor Services had been sold came as a complete surprise to almost everyone. The shock soon turned to anger and a feeling that those at the top had deserted the big Northumbria family and thrown them into the hands of a bus group with a ruthless reputation. Though the sentiments were justifiable, the reality was somewhat different. When chairman David Monaghan announced he wished to stand down for personal reasons in 1994, sale of the Proudmutual Group was the only option. Kentish Bus was the problem, having become so successful that its net worth meant purchase of the Proudmutual Group by remaining directors Tony Kennan and John Fickling (Finance Director David Simon had left the company in 1991) was impossibly expensive. British Bus had been set up in 1992 and pursued an active policy of company purchase thereafter. They were immediately interested in the Proudmutual Group and a deal was quickly agreed to with the sale being concluded on 2 July 1994. Steve Noble, who had joined Northumbria in 1987 as its Operations Manager under Tony Kennan, became the new Managing Director. Noble had joined NBC in 1972 with experience at South Wales, Ribble and Southdown and having worked under Tony Kennan for seven years was well qualified for the new role. The new Engineering Director was John Greaves, previously Northumbria's Operations Engineer, having also worked his way through the NBC since joining in 1975. The role of Finance Director, vacant since 1991, was now filled by Northumbria's Management Accountant Gail Hindmarsh. While former Engineering Director John Fickling departed, the previous Commercial Director Tony Kennan remained with the company as Chairman. There was much nervous anticipation of what changes British Bus ownership would bring and there was not a long wait to find out.

The new Managing Director had been told that the previous year's pre-tax profit of £750,000 had to be increased to £3 million in year 1. David Martin became the main liaison between British Bus (led by Dawson Williams) and Northumbria. Martin and Noble set about the seemingly impossible task of returning a record-breaking profit. Everything across the company came in for ruthless scrutiny, even looking at individual journeys on services and cutting waste wherever possible. Within weeks the first changes came. Coaching was abandoned almost completely, leaving only ten vehicles for National Express work. This meant the disposal of half of the coach fleet along with significant redundancies among driving, engineering and travel shop staff. Northumbria's first coaching manager, Joanne Barber, was made redundant. Northumbria's ABTA accreditation was also dropped, meaning local travel shops saw holiday bookings dry up.

Marketing stopped almost immediately, profit-related pay was introduced, engineering costs came under much tighter controls and overheads were cut wherever possible. One of the lesser effects in terms of cost saving, but one of the more disappointing, was that most of the family-friendly extras for which Northumbria was by now famous were discontinued. Exhibition bus 20 and open-toppers 500 and 555 were all sold and a depressing advert in the first British Bus era *Herald* offered the famous Northumbria bouncy castle bus free to a good home.

The bus fleet British Bus inherited consisted of 334 vehicles made up of ten Bova coaches, thirty-seven Leyland dual-purpose coaches, seventeen Optare Deltas, forty-five Leyland Olympians, three Leyland Atlanteans, eleven Daimler Fleetlines, fifty-two Bristol VRs, fourteen Bristol LHs, fifty-one Leyland Nationals, fifty-two Metroriders, forty-one Sherpas and one Iveco minibus. There were also two Carebus contract Leyland Nationals and four Bristol LH driver training buses. Fleet age had suffered badly during the recession years and as a result of lack of investment in new vehicles average service bus age now stood at 11.4 years – much of the fleet was life-expired and in need of replacement. Seven Mercedes minibuses were immediately transferred from subsidiary Stevensons as 962–8 (H801–3 SKY, G174 YRE, G175 DRF, F836/5 BCW) and joined Iveco minibus 961 (E329 EJR) and Metrorider 828 (E676 DCU), which were sourced from former Proudmutual subsidiary

Northumbria was bought by British Bus in July 1994 and seven Mercedes-Benz minibuses were quickly transferred from subsidiary Stevensons. Reeve Burgess-bodied 963 (H802 SKY) was on a Guide Post–Ellington service in Ashington during October 1995. (John Carter)

In July 1994 Leyland National 712 (GOL 399N) was given an overhaul and converted into a mobile training classroom at a cost of £25,000. Renumbered as 90 and re-registered to GSU 347, the new unit featured a fault simulator and video console for advanced driver training. (Steve Johnson)

R&M at Hexham after it had been closed on 29 October. These transfers along with service trimming and some contract losses allowed thirty-one buses (two Leyland Leopard, eleven Bristol VR, nine Leyland National and nine Sherpa) to be withdrawn within the first week of British Bus ownership.

New vehicles ordered by Proudmutual were already in build and on Monday 10 October 1994 a fleet of eight Northern Counties Palatine 2-bodied Volvo Olympians 370-7 (M370–7 FTY) entered service at Hexham dedicated to route 602. These new buses were to the usual Northumbria standard with full DPTAC features and high-backed blue seating. Some journeys used Customer Service Assistants on them to aid passengers. The uplift in passenger numbers on the route was immediate, just as Optare Deltas had improved numbers on Ashington–Newcastle services when transferred there in 1993.

With the first year profit target met, early in 1995 an announcement was made that £3 million would be invested in fifty-six new buses for Northumbria. It was to be another year of mixed news for the company. Gallowgate depot had closed in November 1994 and soon Whitley Bay joined it with services being transferred to Blyth depot in May 1995. In both cases redundancies resulted from the efficiency savings, and there was anger that the news of Gallowgate's closure had been revealed in the *Evening Chronicle* before staff had been told. As the first of thirty-three new Optare Metrorider minibuses (859–891) arrived in July 1995, many bus services across the network that had previously been worked by full-sized vehicles were transferred to minibus operation. This led to ill feeling among drivers as many

Route 602 received another upgrade in 1994 when the final vehicles ordered by Proudmutual were delivered. The eight Volvo Olympians with Northern Counties bodywork initially used Customer Service Assistants to boost passenger numbers. 371 (M371 FTY) turns onto Grainger Street fully branded for the route. (Author's collection)

By the end of 1996 there were nearly fifty of the later Optare Metrorider buses in the fleet. Many previously double-deck routes were now being operated by the type, as here with 886 (N886 RTN) on service 447 at Blyth bus station. Morpeth was by now only served by two buses per hour from Blyth. (Les Simpson)

were forced to accept minibus pay rates. The British Coal contract to train redundant miners also ceased and so the training school was heavily cut back with fewer driving instructors and just three vehicles – Bristol LHs 87 and 89 along with new mobile training classroom 90 (GSU 347), converted from Leyland National 712. HGV training also ended.

Chairman Tony Kennan, the true innovator behind much of what is now the Northumbria legacy, left the company in April 1995 having taken a more backseat role in the months since the British Bus takeover. He, along with former Engineering Director John Fickling, had acquired the Moor-Dale luxury coaching business from British Bus in November 1994 along with Northumbria's Omega and Eurotours contract work. An unwelcome ghost from the past was the reappearance of competition on the Blyth–Newcastle corridor from 9 May 1995, not this time from Target but instead more remarkably from ex-Northumbria staff who had previously worked on the X1 anti-Target rota. Trading as Premier Travel, their PX1 service was soon matched by a Northumbria EX1 service which even used conductors for a period. A repeat of the protracted Target war was clearly not going to be tolerated and Premier withdrew local services on 24 April 1996 to concentrate on coaching. For most of this period customer numbers for both operators were not helped by the complete redevelopment of Haymarket bus station in Newcastle, this only being completed on 2 April 1996.

A change of overall ownership had meant the previous preference for DAF vehicles was replaced with one for Scania buses and bodywork by East Lancashire. When the new large buses arrived in September 1995 it was in the shape of 281–90 (N281–90 NCN) Scania L113

Six short Leyland National suburban coaches were transferred from Kentish Bus in 1989. The group spent time as anti-Target vehicles and on the M64 Riverside Express route. By 1996 only three remained and in April of that year 722 (XPD 233N), by then twenty-two years old, had only a couple of months left as it leaves the new Newcastle Haymarket bus station for Dinnington. (Steve Johnson)

Newcastle Busways was again the source for second-hand double-deckers in 1994 with three 1977 Alexander-bodied Leyland Fleetlines. 506 (OCU 812R) shows the characteristic Tyne & Wear PTE nearside staircase in this 1996 view as the bus prepares to head for Newbiggin on the direct service 434 from Newcastle Haymarket. (Steve Johnson)

single-decks with East Lancashire European bodywork. They and the thirteen Scania N113 double-deckers with angular East Lancashire Cityzen bodies that followed them in January 1996, 381–93 (N381–93 OTY), were all pleasingly still supplied to Northumbria interior specification complete with high-backed seats in the original blue moquette. All the new buses went to Blyth. New buses meant lots of withdrawals and disposals of older stock and by mid-1996 average fleet age in the service bus fleet had been cut from 11.4 to 9.3 years, very similar to that just prior to the recession at the start of 1991. This number was helped further by cascading older buses into subsidiary fleet Hunters of Seaton Delaval. This long-established operator had been acquired by Proudmutual just days before the British Bus takeover and soon became a low-cost unit where life-expired stock could be transferred to win contract work at minimal cost. These buses were painted brown and cream and carried HUNTERS fleet names in red working predominantly in the Whitley Bay, North Shields, Cramlington and Tynemouth areas.

As 1996 drew on it became apparent to Northumbria Managing Director Steve Noble that some very serious problems in terms of cash flow existed more widely in British Bus, causing for example vehicle availability to suffer as spare parts did not arrive quickly. Easter of that year brought the astonishing sight of an HMRC inspector standing in Jesmond depot demanding either a cheque for unpaid taxes or buses would be seized in lieu.

British Bus invested in full-sized vehicles for the fleet, but now Scania vehicles with bodywork by East Lancashire were favoured. Scania East Lancashire single-decks arrived in 1995 and 285 (N285 NCN) of the first batch of ten is leaving Blyth for Newcastle via Cramlington in 1996. (Steve Johnson)

Last of thirteen Scania East Lancashire Cityzen double-deckers delivered in 1996, 393 (N393 OTY) is passing Gosforth Regent Centre with service X11 from Blyth. (Author's collection)

Leyland Olympian 401 (SPY 201X) was an unpopular vehicle at Ashington depot and unkindly nicknamed the depot Lada, after the much-derided contemporary Soviet car manufacturer. It is seen in the old bus station in 1996. (Steve Johnson)

Ashington bus station was rebuilt during 1996 with new stands off Lintonville Terrace. Plaxton-bodied Leyland Tiger 243 (B265 KPF) is seen in 1998 working service 420 to Alnwick having been transferred away from Hexham in 1995. (Author's collection)

Hunters of Seaton Delaval was acquired in 1994 and soon became a low-cost contract unit using elderly Northumbria vehicles. 87 (CPT 738S, formerly 540) and 83 (BPT 917S, formerly 526) are seen at the former Curtis depot in Dudley. Both would return to the main fleet when Hunters was closed, with CPT 738S being the final Bristol VR to be withdrawn in 2001. (Steve Johnson)

On 1 August 1996 Northumbria was sold once again, this time to the Cowie group, as the former British Bus empire collapsed around them in spectacular fashion, its chairman Dawson Williams having been jailed on charges of corruption. Neither David Martin, formerly of British Bus, nor any of the Northumbria directors were implicated in any of the corruption and so continued in post under Cowie with Steve Noble still the Managing Director. The change of ownership therefore meant very little visible change to the company. At least at first.

The fleet at Cowie takeover had fallen to 285 buses, made up of ten Bova coaches, thirty Leyland dual-purpose coaches, seventeen Optare Deltas, ten Scania single-deckers, forty Leyland Olympians, thirteen Scania double-deckers, three Leyland Atlanteans, eleven Leyland Fleetlines, twenty-seven Bristol VR, ten Bristol LH, fifteen Leyland Nationals, seventy-six Metroriders, sixteen Sherpas and seven Mercedes minibuses. In addition there were three driver trainers (two Bristol LH and one Leyland National), two Carebus vehicles (701 and 702) and a further twenty-four buses working from the Dudley depot of the Hunters subsidiary. New vehicles were on order and a further batch of ten Scania single-decks arrived in August 1996 as 271–80 (P271–9 VRG, P814 VTY) with allocation split between Blyth (275–80) and Jesmond (271–4 for Cramlington services). Cowie was a much bigger bus group, having also purchased the North East Bus group of companies shortly before British Bus. This had the interesting effect of returning Northumbria and the company it had been formed from, United Automobile, into common ownership but also meant that second-hand vehicles could be transferred to and from a much wider selection of sources.

Following a full rebuild of Ashington bus station and depot between 15 July and 31 October 1996, the changes in 1997 began in Berwick, the scene of so much fighting in earlier years where bus station facilities and the depot were abandoned on 2 February in favour of a shared site at the Tweedmouth DoT Testing Station. This move caused many problems as there was little parking and at 2 miles distant was a long walk on a wet day for a break. Relations with Lowland had thawed in Berwick almost from day one of British Bus operations with a joint travel shop being established between the two rival operators from July 1994, and Lowland withdrawing most of its competitive services in the town from 1995.

More vehicles arrived in 1997 including new bus-seated Volvo Olympians 401–10 (P401–10 CCU) that were launched at Newcastle Arena in April before being put to work on Coast Road services 306 and 356. Second-hand Leyland Tiger coaches replacing ageing Leyland Leopards were Duple 320–bodied 202 (XSV 689) and Lasers 219–22 (TSU 636, 869 SVX, YOT 607, VAY 879) that entered service at northern depots in June 1997. A further launch was held jointly with Stagecoach Cumberland on 13 October 1997 for a batch of new route-dedicated Plaxton-bodied DAF SB3000 coaches on the service 685 using 291–5 (R291–5 KRG). This allowed further Tigers to be transferred to Alnwick and Morpeth to improve service 505 and X18. Ashington received four more DAF SB220 in the form of 268/9 (F701/2 ECC) from Crosville Wales and 798/9 (L532/3 EHD) from Arrowline in August 1997, the latter two having Ikarus bodywork. The final five surviving Sherpas (916/8/28/9/31) were renumbered 971–5 in July 1997 to allow for more new Metrorider arrivals to be numbered and these were delivered as 902–14 soon afterwards.

Hunters subsidiary was closed down on 3 August 1997 after poor trading results, with some vehicles being reabsorbed into the main Northumbria fleet and others being disposed

Eleven more Volvo Olympians with Northern Counties bodywork, but with bus seats, arrived in 1997 for Tynemouth and North Shields services. 412 (P412 CCU) is leaving North Shields for Newcastle on the half-hourly service 356 in 1999. (Steve Johnson)

Scania East Lancashire Cityzen 385 (N385 OTY) is seen about to leave Blyth in 1996 for Newcastle via Whitley Bay on service 308, which was worked jointly with Go-Ahead Northern subsidiary Coastline. (Steve Johnson)

Newcastle's rebuilt Haymarket bus station was completed in April 1996 and this view shows the new layout with buses of Coastline and Stagecoach Busways joining Northumbria's 287, 570 and 414. (Robin Trinder)

Despite the take-over of several local independents, very few of their vehicles were ever operated by Northumbria. One exception was Plaxton-bodied Leyland Tiger 250 (EDZ 215, formerly RMO 203Y,) acquired with the business of Hunters of Seaton Delaval. (Steve Johnson)

Four Duple Laser-bodied Leyland Tigers arrived from Maidstone & District and proved popular with passengers on the 505 service. 222 (VAY 879, formerly A182 MKE) leaves Alnwick in July 1997 one month after entering service. (Steve Johnson)

of. The training fleet contracted again and the last two Bristol LH trainers were replaced with two Leyland National 2 9991/2 (RDC 736X, UBR 110V) early in 1997.

Behind the scenes Cowie's Chief Executive Gordon Hodgson was known to dislike the multitude of individual subsidiaries liveries, preferring instead a uniform corporate image. From November 1997 this desire was realised as a new turquoise and cream group livery was unveiled along with the name of ARRIVA. Subsequent deliveries and repaints would all be in the new corporate colours and the Northumbria livery was to be no more, but not before one last vehicle – the first low-floor DAF SB220 saloon with Plaxton Prestige bodywork for the fleet – was delivered in the old livery as 701 (R701 KCU). As 1998 dawned Northumbria Motor Services was just holding on in name but Arriva livery was being applied to new buses (Metroriders 915–23) as well as second-hand arrivals (Leyland Tigers 213–8 YSU 896, XSV 691, YSU 870–1, F188/9 HKK). The Sherpa and the Leyland National were now extinct in the fleet. Optare Metrorider 923 (R923 JNL), delivered in February 1998, would turn out to be the very last bus to enter service for Northumbria Motor Services as plans were soon revealed that subsidiary names were to be changed too. On Thursday 2 April 1998 Northumbria Motor Services was renamed Arriva Northumbria and a remarkable twelve-year existence was over. The final *Northumbria Herald*, still edited by Bruce Hugman, who had been the inspiration behind both original livery and identity, arrived with staff in 1998 and carried a reflective piece about the history of the operator. It had been 4,225 days of highs and lows in which Northumbria Motor Services brightened and changed the travelling habits of the Northumbrian public, as well as the industry more widely.

Delivery of newer buses meant Leyland Olympian 304 (F304 JTY) could be transferred to Berwick depot in 1997. It is approaching journey's end in Newcastle on a service 501 from Bamburgh, which it will have worked from Alnwick due to low bridges further north. (Author's collection)

Competition in Berwick with Lowland ended in 1995. By July 1997 the town centre depots were closed, travel shop boarded up and a general air of dilapidation hung around the bus station where once buses were leaving every few minutes. 1977 Bristol VR 531 (BPT 924S) is ready to leave for the afternoon school bus to Wooler. It would be withdrawn three days later. (Steve Johnson)

The final batch of Optare Metroriders were delivered in two halves with those up to 914 arriving in Northumbria livery. 908 (R908 JNL) has the fine backdrop of Bamburgh Castle behind it as it heads for Berwick. (David Beilby)

Two Ikarus-bodied DAF SB220 buses were acquired from Arrowline in September 1997 and became the last second-hand buses to receive Northumbria livery. 799 (L533 EHD) is seen in Shilbottle working service 420 from Ashington to Alnwick. (David Beilby)

Service 685 between Newcastle and Carlisle, worked jointly with Stagecoach Cumberland, was relaunched in September 1997 using a fleet of new DAF SB3000 coaches with Plaxton bodies, all buses using a common route-branded livery. 291 (R291 KRG) is seen in Hexham bus station after being renumbered 1201. (Author's collection)

The final bus to be delivered painted in Northumbria livery was low-floor Plaxton Prestige-bodied DAF SB220 701 (R701 KCU), which arrived in November 1997. It is being rescreened for a service 42B to Cramlington ahead of ex-Crosville Wales Optare Delta 268 (F701 ECC) in March 1998. (Steve Johnson)

Six former Maidstone & District Plaxton-bodied Leyland Tigers entered service in February 1998, but by now corporate Arriva livery was specified. 216 (YSU 871, formerly E187 XKO) sits in Morpeth bus station shortly after entering service. (Steve Johnson)

The final bus delivered to Northumbria Motor Services, albeit in Arriva livery, was Optare Metrorider 923 (R923 JNL) at Hexham depot in February 1998. Two months later on 2 April 1998 the company was renamed Arriva Northumbria. (Author's collection)

6

EPILOGUE

A detailed account of the events following the end of Northumbria Motor Services on 2 April 1998 is beyond the scope of this book, but a brief summary may be of interest.

Administratively Arriva were quick to change to their corporate structure with head office moving from Northumbria's former offices at Portland Terrace in Jesmond to a new corporate headquarters in Doxford Business Park, Sunderland, on 14 September 1998. Soon after the operations of Arriva Northumbria, Arriva Durham County and Arriva Teesside were merged as Arriva North East, all under the control of former Northumbria Managing Director Steve Noble. These actions effectively reformed almost the entirety of the old United Automobile Services operation, as it had been before 1986. The final step in the process came in November 2002 when Scania 383 (N383 OTY) became the final vehicle to be repainted out of Northumbria livery and into Arriva colours.

A closing fleetlist summarising the buses transferred to Arriva Northumbria is given in Appendix 2. Autumn 2000 saw the final Leyland Leopard (239 – SND 296X) and Fleetline (596 – PRJ 492R) be withdrawn. Bristol VRs' numbers had been cut to 9 by the start of 2000; eight of these were withdrawn in July 2000, leaving only 540 (CPT 738S) at Hexham, which continued until withdrawal in April 2001. The last of the original batch of MCW Metroriders 801–845 departed in 2000 while the 'Habitat' Olympians 303–312 were sold in 2003. August 2005 saw the end of the Optare Delta in Northumberland as 255 (G255 UVK) was withdrawn and in the same month the final four Leyland Olympians, 407–9 (C260-2 UAJ) and 302 (C264 XEF), were stood down, with Northumbria's launch vehicle C264 XEF taking the honour of being the last former United bus to be withdrawn.

The real survivors against the odds were the elderly Bristol LH single-decks. Dating from the 1970s and originally intended to have a service life of under ten years, six of the original thirty-eight survived into Arriva ownership, by now renumbered as 191–6. 1976-built 624/191 (NGR 685P) managed to achieve a remarkable twenty-three years in service before withdrawal in November 1999. Four made it into the new millennium with the final two, 633/193 (LPT 701T) and 638/196 (AFB 593V), being withdrawn in August 2000, by which time raucous 'stottie-boxes' had been rattling around Northumberland's roads continuously for thirty years.

Bristol LH 624 (NGR 685P) was a real survivor. It entered service at Wooler depot with United in February 1976. It survived a depot fire, an onslaught of new minibuses, the hilly terrain and several changes of ownership to withdrawal in November 1999 by Arriva Northumbria. It is in Rothbury during 1997, waiting to work another school contract. (Steve Johnson)

Final Bristol LH to be withdrawn was 638 (AFB 593V) in August 2000. It is seen in earlier days passing the entrance to Chillingham Castle on a service 470 from Wooler. (David Beilby)

Routes and infrastructure have perhaps seen the most dramatic changes, with the rural north and west taking the brunt of these changes over the last twenty-five years or so. Berwick operations, previously the scene of so much competition, were sold to local independent Perrymans along with six Optare Metroriders in October 2002. No evidence of the bus station or depot now remain. Alnwick operations had contracted such that the bus depot was closed (and later demolished) in January 2010, but the logistics of running services to Berwick from Ashington depot over 50 miles away meant an outstation was reopened in September 2013. Morpeth bus station was finally rebuilt but the town bus depot was demolished in October 2003. Only four Arriva services now operate north of Morpeth – remnants of the old 505, 501, 420, X18 and 516. In the Tyne Valley, following competition with Go-Ahead Northern, the bus depot at Hexham was sold in March 2010 and the bus station now lies out of use. Only the former service 685 between Newcastle and Carlisle remained in Arriva hands but this final route in the area was fully transferred to Stagecoach during 2023. The 1996 bus depot at Ashington is now deserted and operations are centred at a new site away from the town centre. It was revealed in 2021 that Jesmond bus depot had also been sold. This leaves the rather bleak picture that, by the end of 2022,

Many vehicles saw life with other operators after their days with Northumbria were over. Perhaps none so different as Leyland Olympian 309 (F309 JTY), seen here in 2016 at the Golden Gate Bridge in San Francisco after conversion to open-top – a far cry from its days working endless Newbiggin–Ashington–Bedlington–Newcastle services! (Chris Martin)

only Blyth depot will remain of those used by Northumbria Motor Services. The scale of rural service cuts that have been echoed across the country mean the fleet strength of Northumberland area depots, which was 361 at its peak in 1991, is now only 150 buses.

Legacy is often an almost intangible characteristic to define, but this is most definitely not the case for Northumbria Motor Services. A bold and daring operator, it challenged orthodoxy and conventionality in every aspect of its operations; not just change for the sake of change, but change to benefit passengers and to create an agreeable workplace in which staff would be proud to work. Approaches such as consulting bus users, specifying buses and adjusting routes based on customer suggestions, using buses to the correct specification to reverse a trend of falling passenger numbers, and recognising that positively engaged staff are key to passenger retention were all used extensively by Northumbria long before they became industry standard practice. Northumbria also saw the benefits of remaining ahead of industry developments, for example prohibiting smoking and specifying accessible buses well before legislation mandated it. Almost exactly twenty-five years later, in 2011 as Environmental Manager at Lothian Buses in Edinburgh, I used exactly the same 'hide the new buses until the very last moment' surprise technique to launch Scotland's first hybrid bus fleet. Our buses even had 'Be bold' and 'Be daring' on the side. Imitation, as they say, is the sincerest form of flattery.

Fully restored and always immaculately presented, DAF SB220 Optare Delta 251 (G251 SRG) has been preserved by former Northumbria directors Tony Kennan and John Fickling so that future generations may enjoy this most distinctive of liveries. The bus was the first of its type delivered to Northumbria, entering service in November 1989 at Jesmond. (John Carter)

APPENDIX 1

Renumbered Northumbria Fleet
(as it was on 30 November 1986)

Fleet Number	Type	Number Owned
71–2	Bristol FLF	2
101–9	Bova Europa	6
110–2	Bova Futura	2
123–7	Leyland Leopard (coach)	4
130–3	Leyland Tiger	4
155–63	MCW Metroliner	7
201–33	Leyland Leopard (dual-purpose)	33
301–2	Leyland Olympian (coach seats)	2
401–34	Leyland Olympian (bus seats)	34
501–91	Bristol VRT	91
601–38	Bristol LH	38
650	Dennis Lancet	1
701–9	Leyland National 1 (second-hand)	6
730–2	Leyland National 1	3
733–5	Leyland National 2	3
750–74	Leyland National 1	25
775–86	Leyland National 2	12

Notes:
71–2 were driver training buses
601–19 were withdrawn tactical reserve
Seven Bristol RE, two Leyland Leopard and two Leyland National 1 (MCN 837L, NCN 956L) were owned but withdrawn awaiting disposal. These were not renumbered.
650 was a long-term loan from Hestair-Dennis.

APPENDIX 2

Northumbria Motor Services Fleet at end of operations 2 April 1998

Fleet Number	Type	Number Owned
131–40	Bova Futura	10
202	Leyland Tiger (Duple)	1
203–6	Leyland Leopard	4
214–22	Leyland Tiger (Duple/Plaxton)	9
230–41	Leyland Leopard	3
242–50	Leyland Tiger (Plaxton)	9
251–69	DAF SB220 (Optare)	18
271–90	Scania – East Lancashire European (single-deck)	20
291–5	DAF SB3000 (Plaxton – coach)	5
301–2	Leyland Olympian (ECW – coach seats)	2
303–12	Leyland Olympian (Alexander – coach seats)	10
313–22	Leyland Olympian (ECW – coach seats)	10
370–7	Volvo Olympian (Northern Counties - coach seats)	8
381–93	Scania – East Lancashire Cityzen (double-deck)	13
401–9	Leyland Olympian (ECW – bus seats)	9
410–20	Volvo Olympian (Northern Counties – bus seats)	11
504–6	Leyland Fleetline (Alexander)	3
527–91	Bristol VRT	28
592–9	Daimler Fleetline (Northern Counties)	8
624–38	Bristol LH	6
701	DAF SB220 (Plaxton Prestige)	1

Fleet Number	Type	Number Owned
798–9	DAF SB220 (Ikarus)	2
801–45	MCW Metrorider	34
846–923	Optare Metrorider	76
965–6	Mercedes 811D	2
9990–2	Leyland National 1 & 2	3

Notes:

9990–2 were driver training units.

Also in fleet, but withdrawn awaiting disposal, were Leopards 229/31/2/5, Bristol LH 637, Leyland National 2 776, Metrorider 842 and Sherpa 971 (D916 VCN).

For full details of fleet, allocations, types and registration numbers over the years 1986–1998 visit www.northumbriabuses.co.uk